THE LITTLE BOOK OF

HORSE RACING LAW

CHARLES A. PALMER & ROBERT J. PALMER

AMERICAN BAR ASSOCIATION
Defending Liberty
Pursuing Justice

Cover design by Andrew Alcala/ABA Publishing.

Printed in the United States of America.

18 17 16 15 14   5 4 3 2 1

Library of Congress Cataloging-in-Publication Data

Palmer, Charles A., (lawyer) author.
  The little book of horse racing law / Charles A. Palmer, Robert J. Palmer.
     pages cm
  Includes bibliographical references and index.
  ISBN 978-1-62722-502-1 (alk. paper)
  1. Horse racing--Law and legislation--United States. I. Palmer, Robert J.
II. Title.
  KF3989.P35 2014
  344.73'099--dc23

                                                        2014008464

Table of Contents

Acknowledgments

Charles Palmer:

I wish to express my sincere appreciation to my administrative assistant, Kathy Fleming, who read and commented on every page of my submission, and to my friend and colleague, Professor Terry Cavanaugh, for his numerous suggestions which made this a better book.

Robert Palmer:

I wish to acknowledge the support and encouragement of my wife, Summer, who's thoughts, insights, and suggestions on the drafts of this book were invaluable. I would also like to thank my daughter, Georgia, for reminding me that there is joy in every aspect of life.

Preface

Charles A. Palmer

Longo v. McIlmurray, 321 N.W.2d 701 (Mich. Ct. App. 1983)

I grew up around horse racing. I don't recall watching my first race. Early in my life, I remember watching the horses go by on the backstretch of Jackson Harness Raceway. I stood on the cross-pieces of the high fence to peer over at the races going by. At that time, children were not allowed into the grandstand where betting took place. That didn't matter to my father; he was a barn guy, not a grandstand guy. In the chilly fall air, I ran out to watch the horses go by on the track and then headed back into the barn for warmth. Barns with horses are always warm.

Many years later, after law school (1979), I watched my Dad's best horse, Happy Sharon, race in the feature race at Wolverine Raceway. Happy Sharon was one of those unique females who could race the males and beat them. She was racing an excellent group of male horses that night, including the standout, Mighty Phantom. During the race, Mighty Phantom was on the rail in third place when Happy Sharon started to pass. The horses were on the backstretch so it was hard to see them closely from the grandstand (I had graduated to watching horses in the grandstand by then) but Mighty Phantom pulled out near the oncoming Happy Sharon, forcing her to quickly slow down and move farther out on the track. Mighty Phantom went on to win that race and Happy Sharon finished second. Wally McIlmurray, my father's driver, claimed—indeed insisted—that Mighty Phantom had pulled out too late, interfering with the oncoming Happy Sharon. But the judges rejected that claim and ruled the finish of the race "official." In the barn afterward, Wally was irate. He was adamant that somebody should do something about this injustice. So the boy from the backstretch fence was nominated to contest the result before the racing commissioner. How could any sane person not see that interference? Certainly the Michigan Office of the Racing Commissioner was composed of sane people who could see.

The racing commissioner appointed a lawyer who was familiar with horse racing to conduct the hearing. A horse race is filmed from many different angles and all of the angles, even some the track judges had not seen, were available for viewing at the hearing. We watched all of them at the hearing, sometimes several times. After watching all of the film and listening to the testimony of the drivers in the race, the hearing officer ruled that there had been interference and that the interference had affected the outcome of the race. Happy Sharon was adjudged the winner of the race. But horse-racing people are competitive. Mighty Phantom's owner, driver, and lawyer did not agree that there had been interference. They filed suit in the Wayne County Circuit Court, challenging the ruling of the racing commissioner.

The circuit judge was upset that the bettors had been paid as if Mighty Phantom had won while the racing commissioner ruled that the owner of Happy Sharon should receive the winner's share of the purse. So who won the race? The circuit judge thought there should be only one answer. Plus, even if there was interference, the judge didn't believe that the interference had affected the outcome of the race. He reversed the decision of the racing commissioner, reinstating Mighty Phantom as the winner of the race.

Our side was competitive too; plus we also had an inexpensive lawyer—me. We appealed to the Michigan Court of Appeals.

The oral argument of the case on *Longo vs. McIlmurray* was set for a January day in Michigan when heavy snow was predicted. Many of the oral arguments scheduled for that day were being adjourned but not *Longo vs. McIlmurray*. Both counsel were there and ready to make their points. It was not a grudge match but the race was continuing.

The appellate court struggled with the issue of a balance of power between the track judges and the racing commissioner. The circuit court judge thought that the track judges determined facts and the racing commissioner must accept those facts unless there was an abuse of discretion. I argued that the racing commissioner had the authority to do a de novo review of the track judges' findings. The racing commissioner was in a far better position to make a factual determination. The racing commissioner did not have a racetrack and bettors impatiently waiting for his decision. The racing commissioner could view all the films, listen to the testimony of the other judges and the drivers, and listen to the arguments of counsel for both sides before making a factual determination. I argued that the appellate court should respect these different opportunities to make a determination of the facts.

The court of appeals agreed; once again, the result was reversed. In fact, this case was reversed each time it was appealed; Mighty Phantom won before the track judges, Happy Sharon won before the racing commissioner, Mighty Phantom won again before the circuit court, and Happy Sharon won before the court of appeals. The case was appealed to the Michigan Supreme Court but, mercifully, the Michigan Supreme Court refused to grant leave. Happy Sharon won the race and was paid the winner's share of the purse.

While the appeal was pending, my dad sold Happy Sharon to horse-racing investors. She was done with her racing days as a four-year-old; it was time for her to produce more racing stars. She was retired from racing.

About 20 years later, my sister (a track veterinarian) called to say that Happy Sharon was going to be sold at auction. She was getting older and the large breeding farm she was with was "culling" their older mares. My father had died by that time, but we went to the sale and bought Happy Sharon back. We brought her to the farm in Michigan where she had grown up. She had a couple more colts, but mostly she became the friend of my son, Rob, a coauthor of this book, and his wife, Summer. She died there on the pastures she grew up on.

I've always found the horse-racing crowd of colorful, passionate people and the structure and formality of the legal system to be a fascinating combination. In many ways they don't seem to fit. But they do fit because they have to. That's what this book is about; forcing an unruly world of colorful characters into a formal decision-making structure. I've watched this process for many years so I thought I'd tell you about it, as will the kid who loved Happy Sharon so much, my son.

Preface

Robert J. Palmer

I am from a family of horsemen, and throughout my life, this fact has been both a blessing and a curse. I have experienced the awe of watching a field of 20 magnificently manicured three-year-olds break from a starting gate with the hopes of wearing a wreath of roses, and I have stood mouth agape at that thundering herd of million-dollar horseflesh, cracking whips, jockey whistles, and dirt flying by with blistering speed. I have leaned across a homestretch rail to scream, at the top of my lungs, for an amazing, once-in-a-generation filly named Rachel Alexandra close with massive strides to overpower a field of the best-aged horses in the country and win the Woodward Stakes at Saratoga. I have seen Europe's dazzling Triple Crown winner, Sea the Stars, dominate that continent's finest in winning the Epsom Derby. And, I have stood through a long, cold Louisville day with anticipation bordering on nausea, only to watch my daughter's hero, the brilliant race mare Zenyatta, suffer the only loss of her career, to the aptly named Blame, in the Breeder's Cup Classic.

Horses have always dominated my life, and with a grandfather, father, aunt, uncle, and cousins all involved in the horse-racing industry in some form, I can't imagine that it would have ever turned out any other way. I recall with great fondness my boyhood dream of being a cowboy and riding the range, and then, at the age of eight or nine, watching from my front door on a crisp October day as my aunt pulled into the driveway with a truck and horse trailer, from which she unloaded a small painted pony named Thunder. Never mind my mother's protests, or the fact that we lived in the middle of the suburbs. My aunt immediately announced, to my immense satisfaction, that if I was to be a cowboy for Halloween, then I needed a horse. My father immediately went to work on our two-car garage, and soon he had split the garage into one parking

xiii

space and one stall, the pony sharing the garage with my Mom's blue Volkswagen Beetle. I was the coolest kid in the neighborhood that fall, with the coolest Halloween costume.

The horse theme continued throughout my childhood. I took dressage and show-jumping lessons at a local farm, and had very modest success in the show ring. At dinners with my family, racehorses such as Secretariat, Ruffian, and Seattle Slew were often topics of conversation, mentioned in the same breaths as other sporting heroes like Joe Montana, Michael Jordan, and Wayne Gretzky. I spent many weeks during my summer vacations working on my grandfather's farm, tending to the horses that lived there and listening in the evening to the old men, coffee cups in hand, who came to talk to my grandfather about horses. I recall many times falling asleep on the leather sofa in his den, growing tired of the five-hour conversations about the proper angle at which to trim a trotter's hoof, or the appropriate use of bell boots. Then, when finally carted off to bed, I would be covered with cooling sheets won in stakes races by one horse or another.

After graduating from high school, I enrolled in the agricultural technology program at Michigan State University, where I majored in horse management (a two-year associate's degree). It was there that I was lucky enough to meet my future wife, Summer, herself a horse fanatic who had grown up showing Arabian horses. As I recall it now, my life at that time seemed to encompass horses from the moment I awoke in the morning until the second my head hit the pillow at night. I worked at the MSU horse farm most days, feeding and caring for its herd in the mornings, before attending courses on equine nutrition and conformation in the afternoon. Many evenings, I could be found at the racetrack, working as a groom for my uncle, where I helped to paddock the horses before the race and then spent long nights cooling them out after they had crossed the finish line.

Eventually, I went back to school, earning a bachelor's degree in agricultural communications from Michigan State, and then a law degree from the Thomas M. Cooley Law School. I now have an active personal injury law practice with the law firm of Sinas, Dramis, Brake, Boughton, and McIntyre, P.C., in Lansing, Michigan, a firm that has graciously welcomed me into its ranks, and more importantly, into a group of men and women who I could not be prouder to call my colleagues.

In the practice of law, I have come to realize that the principles I learned about horses and horse racing are the same as those that are involved in legal disputes. The world is not always black and white. It is not always a matter of right versus wrong. The practice of law, and the world of horse racing, exists in that gray area, where everything is a matter of perspective. What is best for a horse, or a client, is not always the same as what is best for the racing industry, or the law. It is this area that I hope this book adequately explores.

My wife and I continue to live on my grandfather's farm in central Michigan, and we now have the privilege of raising our daughter there. Our backyard continues to be filled with retired racehorses, and, if my daughter has her way, a pony will soon be added to the herd. It is to my wife and daughter that I dedicate this book.

THE LITTLE BOOK OF

HORSE RACING LAW

Chapter 1

The Epsom Derby

Horse racing got the "derby" name from the Derby Stakes run at Epsom Downs Racecourse in England. The 12th Earl of Derby hosted a party with a horse race in 1779 at the Epsom grounds. The festival and race have taken place since and the derby name has been passed on to the world's great races of three-year-olds. Contrary to American racetracks, which are laid out around an oval, the Epsom Derby is raced down a straight, then around a long left turn (Tattenham Corner), and then down the straight stretch past the Queen's stands. The Epsom Derby is the middle race in Britain's Triple Crown (preceded by the 2,000 Guineas Stakes and followed by the St. Leger Stakes).

Horse racing is full of interesting stories, and one of the most mysterious races in the long history of the Epsom Derby was the 1913 Derby.

King George V and Queen Mary both attended the 1913 Epsom Derby. King George had a horse, Amner, in the big race. Royalty sat in the viewing stand on the outside of the track, while the commoners would watch from the center area. Emily Davison stood quietly on the inside of Tattenham Corner.

Emily Davison was a noted women's suffragist. She had graduated with a bachelor's degree from London University and an honors degree from Oxford. But she was absolutely outraged by the stigma attached to women by being denied the right to vote. Davison had caused much trouble championing her cause in the past, having been imprisoned seven times where she was force-fed while on numerous hunger strikes. She even hid overnight in the parliament building on census day so she could claim her official address as the House of Commons. In 1912, Davison attempted suicide by jumping off the balcony at the prison she was at, but she was saved by netting three stories below. Emily Davison was not one to be trifled with.

As the second group of horses was rounding Tattenham Corner in the Epsom Derby of 1913, Emily Davison ducked under the fence. She had two Suffragette tricolor banners of purple, white, and green under her coat, which she pulled out as she walked onto the track. After letting some of the horses pass her by, she lunged at King George's horse as if to grab the horse. She caught the horse's bridle and caused the horse to do a somersault in the air. The horse, Amner, was okay, and his jockey also walked away, but Davison was on the ground with blood rushing from her mouth. She was rushed to the hospital but never regained consciousness. She died four days later.

Emily Davison's funeral became a publicity event for the women's suffrage movement; ten brass bands and 6,000 women marched through the streets of London. The funeral was one of the first events to be covered by the just-out newsreel cameras.

Amner's jockey, Herbert "Diamond" Jones, walked away from the incident, but he was seriously distressed by it. His career went downhill after the race and he retired in 1923. When Emmeline

Pankhurst, the leader of the suffragists, died in 1928, Jones went to the funeral and left a wreath to the memory of Miss Emily Davison. Jones committed suicide in 1951.

But the incident at Tattenham Corner was not the only mystery of the 1913 Epsom Derby. Emily Davison had interfered with the second group of horses. The first group, which passed by before she stepped onto the track, went on to finish the race, with the favorite Craiganour crossing the finish line about a neck in front of the long shot, Aboyeur. Craiganour and Aboyeur were bumping into each other down the stretch but the crowd paid little attention to it; no derby winner had been disqualified since 1844. In due time, after the weigh-in of the jockeys, the flag was raised, indicating that the race finish was "official." Many of the bookies (Britain at that time did not have pari-mutuel wagering) began paying their wagers. But a rumor was soon confirmed that the judges were considering disqualifying the winner, even though none of the owners or jockeys in the race had objected. Someone, among the three judges of the race, had objected or called the result into question. One of the judges, Major Eustace Loder, was the original breeder of Craiganour. It seems unlikely that Loder would object to the victory of a horse bred and raised on his farm. Lord Rosebery would certainly have been the best known figure of the judges. He was a former prime minister of England whose horses had won the Derby three times. He was very interested in the "formation of character" and had contributed money to the lord mayor's *Titanic* fund before the survivors of the wreck reached land. And therein may lie the answer to the mystery.

Craiganour was owned by C. Bower Ismay. Bower Ismay was the brother of J. Bruce Ismay, the chairman of the White Star Line, the company that had owned the *Titanic,* which sank the year before. As chairman of the board of the White Star Line, Ismay closely supervised the plans for the new ship, *Titanic*. Ismay wanted the

Titanic to have luxury items aboard to compete with the Cunard Lines' RMS *Lusitania* and RMS *Mauretania*, two recently introduced luxury liners. In order to accommodate all his additions to the luxury items aboard the *Titanic*, Bruce Ismay ordered that the 48 lifeboats designed for the boat be cut down to 16, the minimum allowed under English law. The *Titanic* could have used more lifeboats.

The chairman of the board often went on the maiden voyage of new ocean liners. J. Bruce Ismay was on the first voyage of the *Titanic*. Before sighting the iceberg, Ismay had encouraged the ship's engineers to proceed with all due speed to test the speed of the ship. But when the *Titanic* began to sink, J. Bruce Ismay jumped on one of the limited life boats. He was rescued by the *Carpathia*, the ship that picked up most of the *Titanic* survivors. But in the age of yellow journalism, Ismay was not treated well in the British or American press. He was called the "Coward of the *Titanic*." The Ismay name was well known but not well regarded. Did this influence the outcome of the Epsom Derby of 1913? Did Lord Rosebery, a friend of the *Titanic* survivors, object to the victory of the horse owned by Ismay's brother? We can't know for certain, but it sure was a strange race.

A little over a year after the Epsom Derby of 1913, Gavrilo Princip assassinated the heir to the Austro-Hungary throne, the Archduke Franz Ferdinand. British forces invaded the Togoland thereafter. The worlds of those attending the Epsom Derby of 1913 would be forever changed.

Chapter 2

History of the Pari-Mutuel

For as long as there has been horse racing, there has been gambling. Whether it's two kids racing their ponies to the end of a fence, or hundreds of thousands scouring the racing program of the Kentucky Derby, you can be assured that virtually everyone who watches a horse race thinks that they can pick the winner. More often than not, picking that winner involves some form of money wagering.

In the early days of organized horse-racing tracks, the most common form of gambling was through bookmakers, or "bookies." These bookies would often operate what were known as "auction pools." In an auction pool, the rights to each horse or entrant would be auctioned off to the highest bidder. Then, upon completion of the race, the bookmaker would take his cut of the total auction proceeds, and pay the individual holding the ticket of the winning horse with the remainder of the pot. Although this system worked for the bookies, it created problems for large portions of the betting public. Because only one person in each auction pool was allowed to hold the ticket for a particular horse, many prospective gamblers were not able to bet, as they couldn't afford to purchase the ticket for their particular choice in the race.

In 1867, Joseph Oller developed a revolutionary new system for solving these gambling problems in the form of the pari-mutuel wagering system. This new system allowed anyone to place a wager. Rather than betting against the house, as occurs in many casinos, gamblers bet against each other. Under the system, any gambler can make a wager with the track, on any horse the bettor chooses. The system then uses a complex algorithm to calculate the odds on any individual horse. At the exact moment the race starts, the system locks and determines the final odds for each entry. The algorithm accounts for a percentage to the house, which is often referred to as the "house take," and then calculates the odds for each horse by assuring that the money bet on the non-winning horses is enough to allow the track to pay the winning wagers. Under this system, the track is always assured the same percentage take. Gamblers are betting against each other because the wagers placed on any one particular horse will conversely affect the odds for the other horses in the race.

As the new system began to catch on in Europe, it was witnessed by Meriwether Lewis Clark Jr. Clark was the grandson of General William Clark, of the Lewis and Clark expedition. Clark's mother was Abigail Prather Churchill, of the well-known Churchill family of Louisville, Kentucky. When Abigail died during Clark's childhood, Clark was sent to live with the Churchill family, and his exposure to the Kentucky horse-racing world soon led him to develop the idea of founding a racetrack in Louisville. Clark's plan was to erect a grand racecourse patterned after the most famous venues in Europe, including the Epsom Derby in England and the Prix de l'Arc de Triomphe in Paris. When Clark returned from Europe and founded Churchill Downs, the home of the Kentucky Derby, in 1875, he brought with him this new system of pari-mutuel wagering.

The new system did not immediately catch on in America as it had in Europe. In fact, by 1899, Churchill Downs, which was facing significant financial difficulty, had abandoned the system after facing pressure from the bookmakers who were being displaced by the new system. However, in 1902, the track was purchased by a syndicate headed by Colonel Martin J. "Matt" Winn. Winn immediately set about renovating the track, and in 1908, Winn sought to reinstate the pari-mutuel system in time for that year's running of the Kentucky Derby.

However, in reinstating the system, Winn had a problem. A Kentucky statute made it a felony to "set up and carry on any machine used in betting whereby money or other thing may be won or lost." Although the statute specifically exempted any persons who sold "French pools on any regular race track during the races thereon," it did not specifically exempt the purchase of those wagers.

Based on this statute, a group led by then Louisville mayor James Grinstead filed a petition with the Jefferson County court seeking an injunction against the system's use. When Jefferson County Circuit Court Judge Samuel Kirby denied the motion, Grinstead's group appealed to the Court of Appeals of Kentucky, that state's highest court. Agreeing with Kirby, the court of appeals denied the petition, noting that "the Legislature intended that the selling of combination or French pools on any regular race track during the races thereon should not be illegal," and therefore, if the selling of the wagers was not illegal, then presumably the Legislature had intended that their purchase should likewise be permissible. Notably, the decision was dated May 6, 1908, one day after that year's running of the Kentucky Derby.

With the blessing of the court, the system soon took off throughout Kentucky and the rest of the United States. Its development was further aided by the invention of the Totalisator machine, a mechanical device that could quickly calculate the advanced algorithms needed to run the system. The first of these systems in the United States were installed at Haileah Park in Florida in 1932 and Arlington Park in Chicago in 1933. The large display boards that posted the ever-changing odds of the Totalisator were soon known as the "tote boards."

Not only did the new pari-mutuel system make gambling easier for the general public, but with the difficulties of calculating odds largely gone, it also allowed tracks to accept increasingly more exotic wagers. In addition to the standard win, place, and show bets, tracks begin offering exacta (picking the top two horses in a race in order), trifecta (picking the top three horses in order), and superfecta (picking the top four in order) wagers. Furthermore, they could easily except multirace wagers, such as the daily double, wherein bettors must pick the winners of two consecutive races; the triple, wherein bettors must pick the winners of three consecutive races; and what many consider the toughest wager in racing, the pick-six, wherein gamblers must pick the winners of six straight races.

In many ways, the pick-six is considered the ultimate gamble. By requiring the pick-six gambler to pick the winner of six consecutive races, it ensures that its winners don't just get lucky on one particular horse, but rather it tests the gambler's skills across virtually the entire day's race card. The wager further entices gamblers because its purse, or "pot," is held separate from the other monies wagered on each individual race. In fact, the bet is so difficult to win that often no individual bettor will have a winning ticket for that day's pick-six wager. In such a case, the pick-six pool will "roll over" to the pick-six pool for the next racing date at that particular track, meaning that in some cases, the money held in the pick-six pool can reach well into the millions of dollars.

As can be expected when such large amounts of money are on the line, any suspicions of dishonesty or foul play in pick-six betting will often wind up being litigated in the courts. One such example occurred in the case of *White v. Turfway Park Racing Ass'n*, 909 F.2d 941 (1990).

On March 23, 1988, Albert White and his gambling partner, Leon Hughes, placed a $216 wager on the pick-six at Turfway Park, in northern Kentucky. This particular wager required bettors to pick the winners of races three through eight. White and Hughes correctly picked the winners of five of the six races, but in race number seven, the horse on which they wagered finished second to a horse named Matter of Time.

Several days after the race concluded, White discovered that the workout time for Matter of Time may not have been posted and made available to the public, as required under Kentucky law. Workout times are important in thoroughbred racing, as they help to inform the betting public about how well an individual horse is training, as well as confirming that the horse has remained in physical racing shape since its last start. Believing that Matter of Time should have been disqualified for failure to post a workout time, and that the horse on which he bet should have been moved from a second-place finish to first, White brought suit against the racetrack.

Testimony taken during discovery revealed that the workout times for horses racing at Turfway Park were typically posted on the track's video monitors. Matter of Time's trainer, Earl Teater, testified that on the night in question, he had provided Gary Smith, the paddock judge, who is responsible for posting the workout times, with a copy of the workout time for Matter of Time. Smith testified that he found the workout time on his desk sometime after the third race of the day, and that he immediately called the track's video-monitoring contractor, Glajour Electronics, and asked them to post the time. Glajour was unable to confirm whether the workout time was ever actually posted.

Furthermore, Albert White's gambling partner, Leon Hughes, who had actually placed the bet, testified that he had considered including Matter of Time as part of his wager because he had been impressed with the horse's speed during his last race. However, because no official workout time had been posted, Hughes apparently was concerned that the horse was not fit for racing. After watching for a workout time to be posted, and not seeing one for Matter of Time, Hughes chose not to include him as part of the wager. However, Hughes also conceded that the track was busy that evening, and that he might have simply missed seeing the workout time being posted.

The federal district court dismissed White's lawsuit, stating that White had not significantly alleged fraud on the part of the track, nor could he prove that the workout time had never been posted. When White appealed, the United States Court of Appeals again dismissed the suit, stating that the district court had properly disposed of the matter. Specifically, it confirmed that White had not put forth significant facts to establish fraud or common law negligence on the part of the racetrack.

Chapter 3

Excluding the Rascals

Barry v. Barchi, 443 U.S. 55 (1979)

Madden v. Queens Cnty. Jockey Club, 72 N.E.2d 697 (C.A.N.Y. 1947)

Marrone v. Wash. Jockey Club, 227 U.S. 633 (1913)

Racetracks have always attracted colorful characters. But sometimes they just don't want those characters around, colorful or not. So when can the tracks exclude patrons? (We're talking about excluding patrons, not licensees like trainers, riders, and grooms, who will be covered later). We all know that patrons cannot be excluded on the basis of race, national origin, or religion but when can patrons be excluded because they're rascals?

In 1907, Joseph Marrone, a garbage man from New York, entered the horse, St. Joseph, in the first race at Bennings racetrack in Washington, D.C. (The Bennings racetrack no longer exists. There is no pari-mutuel horse racing in Washington, D.C., at the present time.) Marrone was listed as the trainer of the horse. At this particular race, St. Joseph was acting strangely before the race and since Marrone was known as a big bettor, the state stewards asked the track veterinarian to take a look at the horse. The veterinarian said the horse seemed to have been drugged. (This was in an era before urine or blood tests for doping were in use.) Nevertheless, St. Joseph finished next-to-last in the race. (If the track veterinarian examined my horse before the race and the horse had been doped, the horse would finish poorly in the race.) But with even the suspicion of doping, the track wanted nothing more to do with the garbage man from New York. He was suspended from entering any more horses at the track and was ruled off the track. The next day, Marrone showed up at the track and purchased a ticket for admission but was not allowed to enter the track. He promptly sued and his case wound its way to the United States Supreme Court.

The English common law precedent for this kind of case was clearly set when James Wood, a bookmaker, had been ruled off the horse tracks in England in the 1840s. Keeping someone from entering the track is more problematic in England than in the United States. In England the horses race at a different track each day. If the authorities at one track in England exclude a patron, the racing will be at another track the next day, so the excluded individual will be able to go to the different track the next day. The mores of horse racing had deteriorated badly in the 1840s. It was discovered in the Epsom Derby of 1844 (the Kentucky Derby of England), a race for three-year-olds, that two of the horses in the race were actually four-year-olds; that the rider of one of the favorites had bet on another horse in the race; and that the most famous bookie on the track had died the morning of the race and his backers had propped up his body in a chair so that the bettors would not discover he was dead until after the race. Lord George Bentinc, one of the leading horse racers of his day, was outraged by all of these shenanigans, and he strongly urged the Jockey Club to rid the sport of these crooks. One of the first abuses they attacked was levanting, the practice of bookies (licensed bookies are legal in England) dishonoring or bolting from their legitimate gambling debts. One of the worst of the offenders was James Wood. The Jockey Club banned him from its racetrack and listed him as an undesirable at other racecourses. Woods showed up at the Doncaster racecourse, purchased a ticket, and was physically thrown off the course by a security officer. Wood was offended and brought suit against the track. Wood contended that once he bought a ticket to the event, he was legally entitled to stay until he was guilty of misconduct. To the racing world, which was trying hard to clean itself up at the time, Wood's argument led to chaos. It meant that the bad actors like Wood could stay at the track until they misbehaved, and then they could move on to another track the next day, where the process would begin anew. The appellate court rejected this argument.

The judges of *Wood v. Leadbitter*, in one of the basic property law decisions of the common law, ruled that the ticket to enter the track was a license and it could be revoked by the property owner at any time. The ticket was not an interest in property, but a contract to admit a person to the land. As such, when Wood was thrown off the course, he could sue for breach of contract, that is, the return of his admission fee, but he was not entitled to stay on the property after the track revoked its permission. The track did not have to catch him before he entered the course; it could still eject him after he had purchased a ticket. *Woods v. Leadbitter* became a basic textbook statement of the common law relating to licenses to enter entertainment facilities. And it was this common law precedent that Joseph Marrone faced went he went before the United States Supreme Court.

Justice Oliver Wendell Holmes wasted few words in disposing of Joseph Marrone's claim that he had a property interest in his permission to enter the track that was not revocable by the track in the absence of wrongdoing on his part. Citing *Wood v. Leadbitter*, Justice Holmes said that a ticket does not create an interest in the land; it creates only a contract to admit the patron to the property. If the contract is breached by improperly evicting the patron without reason, then a breach of contract action will lie. But when the ticket or contract stands by itself, it is simply a contract. Joseph Marrone had a contract but not a right of property. If the racetrack, Aqueduct Raceway, wanted to exclude him from the track, it had a right to do so.

New York Court of Appeals

Owney Madden was one of the prominent bookmakers of the 1930s. He was the bookmaker for Frank Costello and was well connected to organized crime in New York. But Owney, tired of his gangster notoriety in New York, moved to Arkansas to run his gambling operations. On the other hand, Coley Madden (no relation to Owney), was also a prominent bookmaker of a different style. Coley took all the courses he could take in mathematics at Columbia and was described by Red Smith in the *New York Times* as financially sound, socially accepted, and politically entrenched. Aqueduct Raceway would not allow Coley to enter the track because it confused him with Owney Madden. Coley Madden sued; he was not Owney, he was not Frank Costello's bookmaker, and there was no reason to exclude him from the track.

Once again, the bitter legacy of *Wood v. Leadbitter* reared its head. The New York Court of Appeals (the highest court in New York) said that the racetrack could exclude a patron "without reason or sufficient excuse." The court said that under the common law, those engaged in a public calling, such as an innkeeper or common carrier, were required to serve all who sought their services, but private enterprises, like places of amusement, are under no such obligation. Coley Madden, even when he is mistaken for Owney Madden, and even when the trial judge said he was a person of good character, may be legally excluded from the race-track without reason.

Trainers, Drivers, Jockeys, Grooms, and Owners

Although the track has the right to evict patrons without reason, the same does not hold true with licensees such as trainers, drivers, jockeys, grooms, and owners. In 1976, a horse trainer named John Barchi finished second at Monticello Raceway in upstate New York. Two days later, the urinalysis of his horse showed the presence of illegal drugs. Barchi protested his innocence, and he passed two lie-detector tests. Nevertheless, Barchi's license was suspended under the New York Trainers' Rule for 15 days. Under New York law, racetrack personnel could be suspended without a hearing, but they were entitled to a post-suspension hearing if requested. The suspension would take effect immediately, and there was no time limit on when the hearing must be held. A trainer could actually increase his or her 15-day suspension by request-ing a hearing that could take place more than 15 days after the start of the suspension. Barchi appealed all the way to the United States Supreme Court.

The Supreme Court agreed with Barchi that his trainer's license was a property right, protected by the due process clause of the Constitution. Thus, track licensees are protected from arbitrary exclusion from the track where they make their living. Since a trainers' license was a property right, it could not be suspended without due process or a hearing. The Court said that the state could suspend the licenses while they awaited a full hearing, but

21

when the suspension was indefinite, as it seemed to be in Barchi's case, that suspension was a denial of Barchi's constitutional due process rights. Licensees could not be excluded from the course without a hearing of some sort.

Chapter 4

Search and Seizure at the Racetrack

Anobile v. Pelligrino, 303 F.2d 107 (2d Cir. 2002)

Mancik v. Racing Comm'r, 600 N.W. 2d 423 (Mich. App. 1999)

Yonkers Raceway is one of the grand old racetracks of harness horse racing. Founded in 1899 as the Empire City Race Track, Yonkers has gone through a number of owners and changes through the years and is now owned by the five sons of Art Rooney founding owner of the Pittsburgh Steelers. It is the site of some legendary harness races like the Cane Pace, the Messenger Futurity, and the Yonkers Trot. It is also the site of one of the defining events of search and seizure at the racetrack.

Robert Rahner was exercising his horses on the morning of December 9, 1997. As he came off the track after exercising one of his horses, an investigator from the New York State Racing Board asked for his license, which was produced and marked by the investigator. Later that morning, as Rahner returned from the track with another horse, he discovered an investigator from the racing board searching his equipment and trunks. The investigator found injectable penicillin in Rahner's property. The racing board suspended Rahner's license for possessing equine drugs on racetrack property. Rahner objected on the grounds that the search by the racing board violated his rights under the Constitution.

The Fourth Amendment of the United States Constitution prohibits unreasonable searches of persons, houses, papers, and effects, and it further prohibits the issuance of search warrants unless there is probable cause justifying the warrant. In defining unreasonable searches, the United States Supreme Court has distinguished between searching different types of property. The Court has been especially protective of the sanctity of the home and has required warrants for searches of the home in most cases. However, the Court has not been so protective in searches of commercial property. Since highly regulated property, like a racetrack, has a reduced expectation of privacy, the Supreme Court has allowed legally regulated administrative searches to replace the warrant and probable cause requirements of the Fourth Amendment to the Constitution. These "administrative searches" require (1) a substantial governmental interest, (2) that the warrantless searches must be necessary to carry out the regulatory purpose, and (3) that the statute's search program must be circumscribed so as to provide an adequate substitute for the warrant requirement. The first two requirements are usually present for horse-racing searches. The question in most administrative searches on the backstretch of a horse track involves the third requirement, that is, whether the statute or regulation carefully regulates the search so that the government official is limited in his or her personal discretion in conducting the search.

The State of New York passed legislation setting up a state racing commission with the authority and obligation to regulate pari-mutuel racing (New York had only two types of pari-mutuel racing: thoroughbred racing—running horses—and standardbred racing—trotting and pacing or harness horses). The New York State Racing and Wagering Board had general jurisdiction over all pari-mutuel racing and the power to pass rules and regulations in carrying out that authority. The board used that power to pass regulations restricting the possession of drugs, authorizing drug testing of racehorses, and prohibiting the possession or use of certain devices, like hypodermic needles, which can be used to administer performance-enhancing or other drugs to a racehorse. To enforce these prohibitions, the board authorized the inspection of racing facilities and personal property of persons on the racetrack. In addition, licensees of the board—for example, trainers, owners, jockeys, and harness drivers—were required to sign a consent to a search by the board within the racetrack or any space occupied by the license.

Searching the Stables

The New York Racing Board was conducting comprehensive searches of all of the horsemen at Yonkers Raceway on December 9, 1997. The searches were to include the stables, the autos coming in and out of the raceway, and the rooms occupied by the grooms at the track. The search was to be conducted by personnel of the racing board and a drug-sniffing dog.

The Court ruled that the search of Robert Rahner's equipment on a racetrack fell within the warrant exception for administrative searches. The state has a substantial interest in regulating pari-mutuel racing and it is difficult to see how the state could effectively discover and regulate equine drugs at the track if state agencies are required to obtain a warrant for each search. That left the third prong of the test, that is, whether the racetrack searches were carefully circumscribed by regulations. The Second Circuit Court of Appeals ruled that the New York State Racing Board had regulated searches through administrative regulations and directives to such an extent as to limit the investigators' discretion of what and how to search to the purposes of regulation of horse racing at the track.

Searching Dormitory Rooms at the Track

Michael Forte was a prominent harness horse trainer and driver in 1997. He was licensed by the New York State Racing Board for both activities. He was entering the track with his brother-in-law when board investigators checked his license and searched him. Later in the day, investigators searched Forte's room at the track, over his protests. Forte stored equipment in the room, changed clothes there, watched television, and used the room as a bedroom. Forte had a key to the room, which he shared with a groom.

Searching dormitory rooms, even the ones owned by the track, is a different matter. Dormitory rooms are homes to many track grooms and other workers. Privacy expectations are high in homes, private rooms, and even hotel rooms. Dominion and control over the space and the ability to exclude others show a high degree of expectation of privacy. The Second Circuit concluded that warrantless searches of these rooms were not necessary. Since the racing board had the authority to conduct warrantless searches of vehicles, barns, and people on the track, there was an adequate ability to patrol the track and search for illicit drugs without warrantless intrusions into horsemen's private rooms. Searches could be conducted of the rooms at the track if exigent circumstances existed, if business was conducted in one of the rooms, or if the search was directed at felons who were still on probation or parole. But searches of horsemen's rooms on the track without a warrant were unreasonable and prohibited by the Constitution. Any contraband found as a result of these illegal searches had to be suppressed and not used to support the suspension of a racing license.

Consent to Search

Many states now require an applicant for an owner's, trainer's, or jockey/driver's license to consent to a search as part of the application process. But does that "consent" actually constitute a waiver of a horseman's Fourth Amendment rights?

All courts have agreed that a person may consent to a legal or illegal search and, thus, waive any rights to be free of unreasonable searches. But in order to be effective, the consent must be "a product of the individual's free and unconstrained choice." The courts look at the "totality of the circumstances" to make that determination, with the government having the burden of proof to show a free choice.

The court in the *Yonkers* case determined that the consent to be searched, which was required in order to be licensed and to pursue one's livelihood, was not a free and unconstrained choice, at least as applied to a search of the horsemen's residences at the track.

Searches Off the Track

Michigan has moved one controversial step further in searches of horsemen. The Michigan Court of Appeals approved the racing commissioner's search without a warrant, not on the track grounds but off track at the trainer's private property.

Rick Mancik drove Classic Legend, a standardbred racehorse, at Saginaw Harness Raceway on August 1, 1993. A routine postrace urine test indicated the presence of etorphine, a potent painkiller sometimes used to immobilize elephants. Mancik's father was listed as a trainer of the horse so his trainer's license was immediately suspended.

But that left Rick Mancik to replace his father as the trainer of three other horses in his stable and enter them to race at Hazel Park Raceway on August 13 and 14, 1993. Like many harness horse trainers, Mancik did not train his horses at the track but rather at his own training grounds. On August 12, 1993, representatives from the racing commissioner's office appeared at Mancik's private property and searched a barn on the premises, locating illegal drugs, hypodermic needles, and syringes. The racing commissioner indefinitely revoked Mancik's license and excluded him from the grounds of all licensed race meetings for a year. Mancik appealed and the circuit court reversed, finding the search to be an unconstitutional violation of Mancik's rights.

The Michigan Court of Appeals, contrary to the Second Circuit decision, which would come later, found that the consent, which was a condition for a trainer's license, was voluntary and that the voluntary consent covered off-track premises. The search and the suspension were constitutional.

Chapter 5

Drugs in Racing

The use of performance-enhancing drugs in sports, and the many options for deterring and eradicating their use, has dominated national news headlines in North America and abroad in recent years. Major superstars of sport have found themselves the focus and target of investigations by their individual sport's governing bodies, including Alex Rodriguez and Barry Bonds in major league baseball, Lance Armstrong in cycling, and Marion Jones in track and field. The sport of horse racing is no different. The debate over performance-enhancing medications has come under recent scrutiny not only internally but also on a national and even an international level from the media and fans alike. Unfortunately, the systematic use of performance-enhancing drugs in horse racing, and the multitude of jurisdictional authorities who govern the sport, may prove to be a larger hurdle to reform than those seen in almost any other sport.

Drugs have been used to enhance the performance of racehorses since at least the 19th century. In those early years of racing, administering medications, or "doping" horses, was done for various reasons. In some instances, the horse was given stimulants in an effort to make it run faster. However, just as often, a fast horse would be given some form of sedative to slow its competitive drive and "fix" the race, allowing big wagers to be placed on long shots. The medications used to perform these objectives were crude, and they were administered without any real knowledge of how they might affect the horse. In many cases, trainers and veterinarians would use whatever substance they could get their hands on, including cocaine, heroin, morphine, and caffeine. In fact, one story from the early days of racing involved a man nicknamed Railroad Red, a heroin user who frequented the backstretches of racetracks. When trainers were preparing to administer drugs to one of their horses, they would often contact Railroad Red and test the substance on him first. Railroad Red would then report back on the purity and potency of the chosen substance, allowing the trainers to make an educated guess as to the quantity they should give their horse.

As medical science progressed, so too did the options available to trainers and veterinarians seeking to medicate horses for performance-enhancing purposes. The pharmaceutical industry saw a huge bump during World War II and the ensuing years, and, not surprisingly, many of the drugs developed during that time soon found their way to North American racetracks. These new drugs included testosterone; cortisone, which is a steroid hormone used to treat pain and inflammation; Lasix, a diuretic; and clenbuterol, a bronchodilator.

Although racetracks and racing authorities had long sought to end the use of performance-enhancing drugs, with limited success, these new drugs presented a much more complicated problem. Many of these drugs were being administered to heal ailments in horses that would otherwise prevent them from racing. Certainly, the medical treatment of the horses was a legitimate goal that tracks and enforcement groups had to respect. However, at the same time, many of these medications had side effects that helped to enhance performance, and quite often, the legitimate treatment purpose of the drug was merely a ruse for these performance aspects.

Both clenbuterol and Lasix fall into this category of dual-purpose medications, and both have been the subject of long-lasting scrutiny in horse racing. As previously mentioned, clenbuterol is a bronchodilator. In racehorses, it is used to treat respiratory infections and inflammation in the airway. Additionally, it is administered to help horses who are often kept in stalls in dusty barns from developing respiratory infections due to those conditions. However, clenbuterol also has the side effects of helping to increase aerobic capacity and to burn fat and build muscle. As such, many horses that do not necessarily need the drug still have it administered to them on a regular basis. Notably, Alberto Contador, the 2010 Tour de France champion, was stripped of his Tour de France victory and given a one-year suspension for his use of clenbuterol.

Lasix is a diuretic used to treat exercise-induced pulmonary hemorrhage in horses. Just as humans do, when horses engage in intense exercise, they will often bleed in the lungs. The use of Lasix helps to lower the blood pressure of horses, and thus reduce the bleeding that occurs during exercise. However, as a diuretic, the medication also causes a horse to reduce its water content through frequent urination. As such, some critics assert that the medication helps to mask the use of other illegal medications, as the increased urination will flush the horse's system and thereby remove the presence of the other banned substance.

As drugs like clenbuterol, Lasix, and others gained popularity in the racing industry, for both their legitimate and nefarious purposes, the debate over their use, and the penalties that might be attached when those uses ran afoul of the law, began to draw more scrutiny. The problem, however, was that the horse-racing industry as a whole had no centralized authority for enforcing the use of medications. Rather, each individual state in which horse racing occurred was responsible for establishing its own rules and regulations related to the use of medications in competition.

This hodgepodge of rules and regulations across the country set up an interesting dynamic for the individual states and racetracks. The individual states had a responsibility to fans and gamblers to ensure that the racing they put on the track was fair. If the racing was somehow seen as unfair or manipulated, the public trust was likely to wane, and in turn, the revenue made by the tracks and states would drop. However, at the same time, each state understood that if other states provided more lax rules on the use of medication, the horse trainers might be inclined to race in those other states, and the racetracks in the states with tough medication laws would not have enough horses to fill their racing cards. Adding further complication to the matter was the high cost of performing drug testing on the horses, and keeping up with the ever-advancing technology of the tests. It seemed that every time the states developed a test to stop one medication, a new medication was introduced, and a new test had to be developed.

The disparity between the states led the federal government to seek intervention. Several times, the United States House of Representatives considered bills that would nationalize racing regulation. On May 1, 1980, a bill known as the Corrupt Horseracing Practices Act of 1980 was introduced. The legislation stated that it was "a bill to prohibit the drugging or numbing of race horses and related practices, and to amend Title 18, United States Code, to prohibit certain activities conducted in interstate or foreign commerce relating to such practices." With the bill, Congress hoped to establish a national racing commission, through the powers of the interstate commerce clause. However, the bill never made it out of committee.

As the decades drew on, the problem continued to intensify. Horses were being raced with more and more medications in their system. It became so common to run a horse on medication that tracks began administering Lasix on their premises for a small fee. At many tracks, you could find an entire race card without a single drug-free horse. At the same time, several groups noted that the on-track fatality of racehorses was on the rise.

The problem came to a head in 2008. That year, a young colt named Big Brown won the Kentucky Derby. Before the Preakness Stakes, the second leg of the Triple Crown, Big Brown's trainer, Richard Dutrow, admitted that the colt received a shot of stanozolol every month, and had raced with the drug in his system during the Kentucky Derby. Stanozolol, known more commonly by its brand name Winstrol, is an anabolic steroid that can help to cut fat while still building muscle mass. Casual observers of horse racing were aghast, and the sport's image was tarnished in the media. Big Brown went on to win the Preakness Stakes, which was run before the colt was scheduled for his next dose of Winstrol. However, apparently succumbing to pressure from the media, Dutrow promised not to give the horse the medication before the Belmont Stakes, the third and final leg of the Triple Crown. Ultimately, Big Brown was forced to pull up in that race, becoming the first horse with a chance at the Triple Crown to not finish the Belmont Stakes.

Dutrow v. New York State Racing & Wagering Bd., 97 A.D.3d 1034 (2012)

In the years that followed, both horse racing as a sport, and Rick Dutrow in particular, continued to draw fire from critics for the allowance of drugs in racing. By 2012, the state of New York had seen enough of Dutrow's tactics. After a horse trained by Dutrow, named Fastus Cactus, tested positive for butorphanol (an opioid used to mask pain) following a race at Aqueduct in New York, race officials searched Dutrow's barn and found three syringes in his desk that contained the medication xylazine. The racing commission brought charges against Dutrow, and suspended him for 90 days. When Dutrow appealed, the racing commission had seen enough. They fined him $50,000 and suspended his license to train racehorses in New York for ten years. Dutrow appealed, and in a case that made it to New York's appellate courts, the court found that Dutrow's "recurrent misconduct" justified the state's suspension, and the court ultimately upheld the ruling. Dutrow is now serving a ten-year suspension.

It seemed that horse racing had finally started to see the proverbial writing on the wall. In March of 2013, eight states (New York, New Jersey, Pennsylvania, Delaware, Maryland, Virginia, West Virginia, and Massachusetts) announced that they were collectively adopting the Mid-Atlantic Uniform Medication Program. This new program consolidates the rules on drug use within those eight states. The program has listed 24 medications that the states collectively believe are appropriate for therapeutic use in racehorses. Any medication not included on the list is strictly banned, and a positive result with one of these banned medications will trigger harsh penalties that will be imposed in any state that participates in the program. Since that time, California has indicated that it may join the program as well.

Subsequently, in May of 2013, a new bill was introduced in both the United States House of Representatives and the United States Senate by New Mexico Senator Tom Udall. The new bill, known as the Horseracing Integrity and Safety Act, would establish national oversight of drug use in horse racing, by giving authority to regulate drug use in the sport to the United States Anti-Doping Agency (USADA). The USADA currently oversees drug use in multiple sports, including the United States Olympic program.

While it remains to be seen what effect, if any, this new legislation or the compact made by the Mid-Atlantic States will have on eradicating drug use in the United States horse-racing industry, they clearly signal a new dawn in the sport. Even if these actions fail, the sport has been put on notice that it is time to clean up.

Chapter 6

Insurer's Rule

Sandstrom v. California Racing Bd., 189 P.2d
17 (Cal. 1948)

The integrity of the sport of horse racing has always been under assault. It is a highly competitive business where fortunes are made and lost quickly. Recently, that assault has come from performance-enhancing drugs. Numerous laboratories synthesizing all sorts of drugs present an ongoing challenge to those who try to regulate the sport. At times it has seemed that the regulators are losing the challenge. One way to confront the challenge is with increasingly onerous regulations of the sport. In the vanguard of that movement is the "trainer's insurer's rule."

Most racehorse doping cases are discovered as a result of urine testing after the race. That makes it difficult to prove that a trainer, groom, owner, or other party administered the illegal substance. The regulators can search the barns for drug paraphernalia but clever track people are not going to leave that stuff around. Someone has to assume responsibility to get the horse to the race without foreign substances, and the best person to do that is the trainer. Therefore, the racing commissions have adopted a rule

41

requiring the trainer to be the insurer of the horse's condition when the horse comes to the race.

There are two kinds of trainer's insurer's rules: the absolute insurer's rule, wherein the trainer becomes the protector of the horse's condition without any excuses, and the rebuttable presumption trainer's rule, which places the burden of proof on the trainer to show that he or she did not administer the foreign substance. An example of the absolute insurer's rule is the New Mexico rule that states:

ABSOLUTE INSURER:

(1) The trainer is the absolute insurer of the condition of horses entered in an official workout or race and is responsible for the presence of any prohibited drug or medication, or other prohibited substance in such horses. A positive test for a prohibited drug or medication or other prohibited substance or the presence of permitted medication in excess of maximum allowable levels as reported by a Commission-approved laboratory is prima facie evidence of a violation of this rule. The trainer is absolutely responsible regardless of the acts of third parties.

(2) A trainer must prevent the administration of any drug or medication or other prohibited substance that may cause a violation of these rules.

(3) A trainer whose horse has been claimed remains the absolute insurer for the race in which the horse is claimed.

New Mexico Rule 16.47.1.10

An example of the rebuttable presumption rule is Rule 1887 of the California Racing Board:

(a) The trainer is the absolute insurer of and responsible for the condition of the horses entered in a race, regardless of the acts of third parties, except as otherwise provided in this article. If the chemical or other analysis of urine or blood test samples or other tests, prove positive showing the presence of any prohibited drug substance defined in Rule 1843.1 of this division, the trainer of the horse may be fined, his/her license suspended or revoked, or be ruled off. In addition, the owner of the horse, foreman in charge of the horse, groom, and any other person shown to have had the care or attendance of the horse, may be fined, his/her license suspended, revoked, or be ruled off.

The prohibited substances referred to in the California rule are "any drug substance or its metabolites or analogues, foreign to the horse except those substances specifically approved by the California Racing Board." The trainer has to keep track of a lot of substances, for example, peanut butter, worming medicine, chocolate, and so on. That insurer's rule has a long and colorful history.

The Suspension of Seabiscuit's Trainer

Tom Smith is well known as the trainer of Seabiscuit in Laura Hillenbrand's book by that name. Not only did Smith train the iconic racehorse but he was also the trainer for Elizabeth Graham's (Elizabeth Arden's) Maine Chance Farm, the leading racing stable of its day. But horse-racing officials were suspicious of Tom Smith in the 1940s. He had been observed by a track veterinarian spraying the nostrils of one of his horses entered to race. Track officials ordered an investigation. Later, a Jockey Club investigator saw someone (not Smith) spraying something into the nostrils

43

of Magnificent Duel, a horse trained by Smith, who was entered to race. The investigator found in Smith's barn an atomizer that contained ephedrine. Ephedrine is a stimulant and bronchodilator. Even though the person who was observed spraying the horse's nose was not Smith, the racing commission instituted proceedings against him under the trainer's insurer's rule. Smith was suspended for one year in one of the first, and best-known, insurer's rule cases. When Smith appealed, the courts were not sympathetic. Smith later admitted that he knew the horse was getting ephedrine; he said that he took the drug himself for a cold and thought that it would be good for Magnificent Duel, who Smith thought had congestion in his head. But the combined boards of the racing commission and Jockey Club members were not sympathetic. Smith said that he gave it to the horse only for a cold, and Seabiscuit never had a cold. Tom Smith was reinstated and after his suspension, he got Elizabeth Arden's horses back to train and went on from there to win the Kentucky Derby with her farm's horse, Jet Pilot, in 1947.

The Constitutionality of the Absolute Insurer's Rule

The constitutionality of the absolute insurer's rule has understandably been more controversial than the rebuttable presumption. The Maryland Supreme Court and the Florida Supreme Court struck down the absolute insurer's rule (irrebuttable presumption) as unconstitutional. The rule looked like it was on its way to oblivion when the California Supreme Court took up the matter.

A horse trained by W. L. Sandstrom had a positive test result (caffeine) after a race at the Del Mar Race Track in San Diego. After a hearing, the California Racing Board suspended Sandstrom's license for six months. Sandstrom challenged the rule on the grounds that it was an unconstitutional violation of his due process rights, especially when it imposed responsibility on a trainer for the actions of third parties he could not control. Undoubtedly, Sandstrom was encouraged by the Maryland and Florida decisions holding the rule unconstitutional. But the California Supreme Court wasn't buying it. The California court thought that in areas of traditional regulation, the rulemakers could do away with the requirement of proving fault or awareness of wrongdoing. The absolute insurer's rule was held to be constitutional. The trend of holding the rule unconstitutional was reversed. Other courts in West Virginia, Michigan, Arizona, Massachusetts, New Jersey, and Louisiana followed *Sandstrom*. Florida even reversed itself in 1978. Arkansas approved the absolute insurer's rule in dog racing, even for situations in which the dogs are placed in a kennel away from the owners and trainers for two hours before the race. Because the dogs are monitored by television, which the trainers can watch, the Arkansas court upheld the insurer's rule. The most significant aberration, finding the insurer's rule unconstitutional, is the Illinois Supreme Court, which stated, "Administrative convenience is not a constitutional substitute for the rights of individuals."

The insurer's rule is alive and with us today. Trainers must beware.

Chapter 7

Publicity

Advertising has become synonymous with sports. We have grown accustomed to corporate naming of sports stadiums, multimillion-dollar advertising campaigns launched during the National Football League's Super Bowl, and product placement on numerous sporting uniforms. In some cases, even specific parts of a sporting event carry advertising, such as the Pepsi pregame show or the Home Depot halftime report. It is hard to imagine the sport without the advertising. In NASCAR, racecar drivers and their cars have become so closely linked with their corporate sponsors that we would not expect to see the former without the latter.

In some aspects, horse racing is no different. The Kentucky Derby is now presented by Yum! Brands foods, which owns Kentucky Fried Chicken and Taco Bell, among others. Virtually every race of the Breeder's Cup Thoroughbred Championships is sponsored by some corporation, with Dodge Trucks having sponsored the premier race for the past several years.

But in some ways, horse racing has been slow to allow corporate sponsorship and marketing. Although many individual tracks have cashed in on one form or another, the horses, trainers, and jockeys have often been left to fend for themselves in the corporate sponsorship arena. In some cases, they have met stiff legal opposition.

One such battle occurred in the lead-up to the 2004 Kentucky Derby. That year, two separate groups of jockeys sought permission to wear distinct logos and patches on their racing breeches and the turtlenecks worn underneath the traditional racing colors. The first group was led by jockey Robby Albarado, and they sought the right to wear a patch of the Jockey's Guild on the legs of their breeches. The Jockey's Guild helps support jockeys who have been disabled as a result of racing, and Albarado's group sought to wear the patch to bring attention to the Jockey's Guild's cause.

The second group was led by Hall of Fame jockey Jerry Bailey and included John Velazquez, Jose Santos, Alex Solis, and Shane Sellers. This second group sought permission to wear "tasteful and traditional" logos that advertised corporate sponsors so that the individual jockeys could attract personal corporate sponsorship.

The problem for both groups was the existence of a rule of the Kentucky Horse Racing Authority, which governs thoroughbred racing in Kentucky. The rule prohibited jockeys from wearing advertising and promotional logos on their racing attire. According to the authority, "advertising, promotional, or cartoon symbols or wording which in the opinion of the commission are not in keeping with the traditions of the turf shall be prohibited." 810 KAR 1:009 (1975).

The dispute between the jockeys and the Kentucky Racing Authority had been simmering for some time. During the 2003 Kentucky Derby, several jockeys had worn the patch of the Jockey's Guild, despite the Kentucky regulation preventing it. In response, racing stewards had fined each jockey $500. Additionally, during the early spring racing meet at Keeneland Park, in Lexington,

Kentucky, jockey Jerry Bailey had specifically been denied the right to wear corporate logos on his racing attire. These denials led the jockeys to request a public hearing on the matter before the racing authority in April 2004. When the racing authority again denied the jockeys the right to wear the logos and patches, and made clear to the jockeys that this rule would be in force during the running of the Kentucky Derby that year, the jockeys collectively filed for declaratory relief, alleging that the rule was a violation of their rights under the First and Fourteenth amendments.

In deciding the case, the court determined that the jockeys' requested relief fell into two separate categories. First, Albarado's group's seeking to wear the patch of the Jockey's Guild amounted to private speech, as the patch was not being used for economic motivation or an advertising purpose but rather to bring attention to a specific cause. Conversely, the court found that the relief sought by Bailey's group amounted to commercial speech, as it was being performed for the sole purpose of economic gain. Accordingly, the court addressed each group's requested relief separately.

Ultimately, the court determined that the Kentucky Racing Authority had no legitimate interest in blocking the protected speech of the two groups. Because the only proffered reasoning was to protect "the traditions of the turf," the court found that no justifiable purpose for imposing upon the substantial First Amendment rights of the two separate jockeys' groups existed. As such, the court issued an order enjoining the Kentucky Racing Authority from prohibiting the jockeys' patches and logos.

While the court's decision in *Albarado et al. v. Kentucky Racing Comm'n*, 496 F. Supp.2d 795 (W.D. Ky. 2004), was relatively straightforward and applied solid legal reasoning, there has been a much bigger debate regarding the publicity rights of the main competitors in thoroughbred racing—the horses themselves. The issue came before the United States District Court for the Northern

District of New York in 1997, in the matter of *Cortez v. CMG Worldwide Inc.*, 962 F. Supp. 308 (N.D.N.Y. 1997), a case that left many questions unresolved.

A number of artists, including Jeness Cortez and Fred Stone, make their living painting images of thoroughbred racing. Many of these images contain famous racehorses, including Cigar, Secretariat, and Ruffian. Cigar won 16 straight races between 1995 and 1996, and retired as thoroughbred racing's all-time leading money earner at the time, with just shy of $10 million in purses won. Secretariat famously won the 1973 Triple Crown. Ruffian was an undefeated three-year-old filly who competed in a match race against 1975 Kentucky Derby winner Foolish Pleasure on national television, and who tragically broke the sesamoid bones in her right front leg halfway through the race—injuries that ultimately led to her having to be put down. All three of these horses evoke fond memories in the hearts of horse-racing fans, and many are inclined to purchase the artwork from Cortez, Stone, and others to commemorate their heroes.

CMG Worldwide Inc. is a corporation that represents various corporations and celebrities in the marketing and use of their likenesses. Among CMG's client base were the owners of Cigar, Secretariat, and Ruffian, and these groups, through CMG, sought to block Cortez and Stone from selling the images of the horses without permission. In early 1996, CMG informed both Cortez and Stone that they must cease and desist from using images of Cigar, Secretariat, and Ruffian in the artwork they were selling.

Knowing that a legal battle was coming, Cortez and the other artists filed a legal action seeking declaratory judgment that CMG had no right to prevent them from selling their own original artworks depicting the horses in question. CMG immediately filed for a motion to stay, as it had already filed against Cortez in Indiana. The specific question at issue was whether a racehorse's likeness was protected under the federal Lantham Act, which protects various individual celebrities' names and likenesses from being used in misleading representation.

The court ultimately denied CMG's request for a stay. It found that although the Lantham Act had been applied to protect human celebrities on numerous occasions, there was no legal history of it being extended to protect any animal. Therefore, the court was not convinced that any entity represented by CMG actually held the right to the animal, and consequently, that it had the ability to protect that animal's likeness through legal means.

The full extent of the rights to publicity for racehorses has not yet been determined, and the issue will undoubtedly be fought further through the court system. Furthermore, with the introduction of the Internet and social media, the marketing of individual horses has taken on a new dimension. It is now common for horses to have their own websites, or even their own Facebook pages, dedicated to their promotion and the selling of their merchandise. As this promotion continues to expand, those seeking to protect their profits will undoubtedly seek redress through the court system.

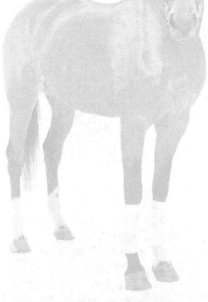

Chapter 8

Kentucky Derby 1968

Kentucky State Racing Comm'n v. Fuller, 481 S.W.2d 298 (Ky. 1972)

The year 1968 was awful. Dr. Martin Luther King Jr. and Bobby Kennedy were assassinated, the Tet Offensive in Vietnam shocked America, and the Democratic National Convention was a mess. Horse racing would be no exception.

The running of the 1968 Derby was relatively uneventful. The 7-to-2, second choice in the Derby, Dancer's Image, came from last place to first, even though his jockey lost his whip. Peter Fuller, a Harvard-educated champion boxer and car dealer from New Hampshire, who owned Dancer's Image, stood in the winner's circle afterward, basking in the glow of a Derby victory. But there were storm clouds on the horizon.

That evening in the little blue-and-white trailer on the back-stretch of the track, racing officials identified a positive test for the prohibited drug phenylbutazone—or bute, as it is known in horse-racing circles. The officials notified track stewards the next morning, and soon the whole world knew that the recent win-ner of the Kentucky Derby would be disqualified for racing with a prohibited substance. Forward Pass, the Calumet horse who finished second, would become the winner after the leader was disqualified.

Bute is an analgesic or painkiller; it is not a stimulant. Like his sire, Native Dancer, and many of his siblings, Dancer's Image had sore ankles. Although the rules of Kentucky and Illinois clearly prohibited racing with any bute in the horse's blood, the rules did not prohibit the use of bute while training the horses the week prior to the race. Dancer's Image's ankles were sore after his previous race and workout, so one of the prominent veterinarians of Churchill Downs, Dr. Alex Harthill, gave him bute on the Sunday before the Derby. Dr. Harthill was a big, friendly vet with a somewhat checkered past. He had admitted giving a horse an amphetamine in Chicago, but his suspension for that incident was overturned on appeal. He was charged with bribery of a public official and stimulation of horses in New Orleans but was subsequently acquitted. Dr. Harthill was not the regular veterinarian of Dancer's Image but was hired by the horse's trainer because he was the "Derby doc" and had a prominent presence at the track.

Bute is not injected; it is a pill that is forced down the horse's throat. Dr. Harthill and other veterinarians were sure that bute would not linger in the horse's system six days after administration, so treating the horse on Sunday was thought to be safe for a race the following Saturday. But there were reasons to doubt the authenticity of the postrace track tests.

A month before the Derby, Peter Fuller had given $62,000, Dancer's Image's winner's purse in the Maryland Governor's Cup race, to Coretta Scott King, widow of the recently slain civil rights leader. Fuller did not publicize his gift, but the television announcer mentioned it at Dancer's Image's next race, the Wood Memorial. Louisville had suffered through acrimonious civil rights struggles, and Dr. King had even threatened to come there to lead protests.

Because of the gift, Fuller received hate mail and he requested extra security for his horse at Churchill Downs but that request was denied. Fuller always suspected that someone had sneaked the bute into his horse but he never had proof. Bute is administered by mouth so it would be relatively easy for a wrongdoer to grind up the pill and pour it over the horse's feed. Fuller claimed that he had found a security guard asleep at the track. A few days later, two reporters from the *Louisville Courier-Journal* went to the track to test this allegation and also found a security guard asleep at the track.

Racetrack stewards are appointed by the state to be present at the races and rule on race complaints. The stewards held a hearing the following Monday. The three stewards on duty for this race were particularly well qualified. The track stewards received the evidence of the positive test and disqualified Dancer's Image. The horse that had finished second in the race, Forward Pass, owned by the Calumet Stables, was declared the winner. Dancer's Image's trainer and assistant trainer were suspended for 30 days under the trainer's rule. But "other issues" were left to be determined by the racing commission.

As the owner of Dancer's Image, Fuller hired two of Kentucky's prominent horse-race lawyers for the racing commission hearing. The relatively new science of chemical analysis of horse saliva and urine would come under fire. Fourteen volumes (2,860 pages) of hearing testimony were produced before the racing commission. But the racing commission agreed with the stewards; Dancer's Image raced with bute; and Forward Pass won the race. But Fuller wasn't giving up.

The racing commission's ruling could be appealed to the Franklin County Court. The county court was not authorized to rehear the case or take new testimony. The court could review only whether the racing commission's ruling was supported by "substantial evidence." Judge Meigs, a decorated war hero, ruled that it was not. The judge thought the chemical tests were not adequate to support the disqualification of Dancer's Image. But there was one last step, one last appellate court, the Kentucky Court of Appeals. The racing commission appealed the decision of the county court.

Fuller objected to the racing commission appealing; after all, the racing commission was a fact-finding body, not a party. But the court of appeals didn't agree. It thought the racing commission could appeal and that there had been "substantial evidence" presented before the commission to show that Dancer's Image raced with a foreign substance in his body.

Finally, it was over. Forward Pass won the 1968 Kentucky Derby. The winner's trophy and purse were given to Calumet, a farm that was facing its own trials.

Dancer's Image raced in the Preakness, and once again, a problem arose. This time his jockey bumped other horses coming down the stretch. A favorite that comes from behind often has problems finding room to race through a packed field, and this time the room just wasn't there. As Bobby Ussery tried to make it, he bumped other horses on the way through. This time there was little controversy about the judge's ruling. Dancer's Image was again disqualified and set back to eighth.

That was enough. Dancer's Image's ankles were sore again. He was retired to stud. Eventually, Fuller sold Dancer's Image. After stops in Ireland and France, Dancer's Image died in Japan in 1992.

Fuller died in 2012. He had a sign on his farm in New Hampshire. The sign showed a picture of Dancer's Image and under it, 1968 Kentucky Derby winner.

Postscript

I went to the 1968 Belmont. Forward Pass was racing for the Triple Crown, so to speak. Mercifully, he didn't win. One of the famous Belmont "outside shooters," Stage Door Johnny, won his first race, the 100th Belmont. Forward Pass finished second.

Chapter 9

African-American Jockeys

They started quickly. African-American jockeys rode 13 of the first 15 Kentucky Derby winners and 15 of the first 28 Derby winners. But then, just as suddenly as African-American jockeys had burst onto the scene, it was all over in the early 1920s. The great black jockeys quit riding or moved away. It was a strange allegory of American racism.

The British brought their love of horse racing to the colonies. George Washington and Thomas Jefferson were horse-racing enthusiasts. The stable hands of slavery were uniquely well suited to excel in the sport. They knew the horses, took care of the horses, and were uniquely qualified to ride the horses when the sport prospered. The great, wealthy families of horse racing—the Phippses, the Vanderbilts, and the Whitneys—all knew that the African-American jockeys, brought up in the scourge of racism, would not cheat their owners for a gambler wanting to fix a race. So, the African-American jockeys rode to fame on the late-19th-century racetracks.

Oliver Lewis, a 19-year-old African-American, rode Aristides, trained by a former slave, to victory in the first Kentucky Derby in 1875. Isaac Murphy was the first jockey to win the Kentucky Derby three times. Murphy won 628 races out of 1,412 mounts, for an incredible winning percentage of 44 percent. He went on to invest in real estate and became the first African-American to own a racehorse. He was buried next to Man o' War in the Kentucky Horse Park.

Willie Simms became the first African-American jockey to venture to the racetracks of England. Simms rode in the style of his friends in the South, crouched forward over the horse's neck with his legs in short stirrups. This was contrary to the upright, long-legged style of the English. The English press made fun of him until he became one of the leading riders of their country. And finally, Jimmy Winkfield won two successive Kentucky Derbies and 2,500 races in his career. He was the last African-American to ride a Kentucky Derby winner.

Just as suddenly as it started, it was all over in the 1920s. Jimmy Winkfield left the United States and moved to Russia, where he won the Moscow Derby. He was doing well there, riding for the Czars until the 1917 revolution. He then moved to France to continue a successful career. But African-American jockeys were done in the United States.

What happened to make these talented African-American jockeys leave horse racing? There is no definitive reason. The immediate reason was that they were being fouled, or run into on the track, and their protests, when they made them, were ignored. Certainly an underlying reason was that they became victims of the new popularity of the sport. Horse racing and boxing became popular and lucrative. The white immigrant jockeys of the North moved to the South to compete for mounts with the established African-American jockeys. That competition was not fair in a strongly racist society. The end of reconstruction, the rise of Jim Crow laws, and the separate but equal decision of *Plessy v. Ferguson* all played a part. Whatever the reason, the rise of the African-American jockeys was over. Jimmy Winkfield was the last African-American to ride a Kentucky Derby winner in 1902, and Jess Conley was the last African-American to ride in a Kentucky Derby in 1921. No more African-Americans rode in the Kentucky Derby for 79 years until Marlon St. Julien did it in 2000. It was a strange interlude.

Chapter 10

Insuring Racehorses

N. Am. Specialty Ins. Co. v. Pucek, 709 F.3d
1179 (6th Cir. 2013)

Valuable racehorses are a risky investment at best. An owner can
remove some of that risk by buying equine insurance. The most
common equine mortality insurance insures against the death of
the horse naturally or by euthanasia. When the owner proposes
to euthanize an insured horse due to irreversible injury or illness,
the owner is usually required to notify the insurance company
and retain a veterinary to treat and salvage the horse if possible.
Many owners want to insure against this additional veterinary
expense so they purchase a rider for their mortality insurance to
cover veterinary care.

Obviously, the insurance companies in this field are concerned
about insurance fraud. Some horses become more valuable as
an insurance claim than they are as a living horse. The insurance
companies try to protect against this fraud by requiring that the
owner immediately retain a veterinarian to try to salvage the horse
but the veterinarians have a tough task spotting the cases where
the horse has been deliberately injured or killed.

Off Duty, a five-year-old thoroughbred, broke two bones (sesamoid) in his front left leg while training at Churchill Downs in October of 2008. The owners notified their insurance company on the morning of the injury. Severely injured legs often cause a horse to excessively stand on the other leg, causing "laminitis" in that other leg, a painful condition that usually requires the horse to be euthanized. Off Duty was removed to Rood & Riddle Veterinary Hospital in Lexington, Kentucky, where it was determined that he would be a candidate for "fetlock arthrodesis," which immobilizes the fetlock or ankle joint. This surgery would not return Off Duty to the racetrack but would keep him alive for other purposes, such as breeding. But there was no evidence that Off Duty would make a desirable breeding stallion.

The owners notified the insurance company that they intended to euthanize Off Duty. One of the owners had visited the horse, videotaped him in his stall, and thought he was suffering. When the veterinarians checked the horse, they found his heart and breathing to be normal and said he was "ambulating well around the stall." The insurance company offered to pay for the surgery but the owners rejected the offer and had the horse euthanized. The owners submitted a payment claim that the insurance company rejected, so the parties were off to court.

The insurance policy excluded coverage for the intentional destruction of the horse except when the horse was destroyed for humane reasons. The policy defined humane destruction as,

The intentional slaughter of a horse:
a.　when the horse suffers an injury or is afflicted with an excessively painful disease and a veterinarian appointed by (North American Specialty's) Managing Underwriter certifies in writing that the horse is incurable and in constant pain, or presents a hazard to itself or its handlers; or

b.   when the horse suffers an injury and (the owners')
appointed veterinarian certifies in writing that the horse is
incurable and in extreme pain, and that immediate destruction is imperative for these reasons without waiting for the
appointment of a veterinarian by (North American Specialty's) Managing Underwriter.

To the court, the answer was simple; no veterinarian certified that
Off Duty had incurable and constant pain. The owner's video of
the horse in pain was irrelevant; the insurance contract called
for a veterinarian's certificate and without it, there was no right
to payment.

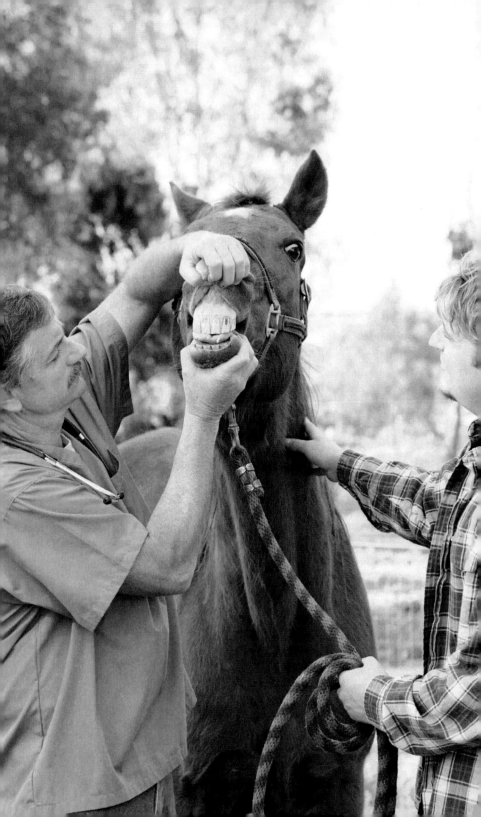

Chapter 11

Horse-Racing Syndicates

Kefalas v. Bonnie Brae Farms, Inc., 630 F. Supp. 6 (E.D. Ky. 1985)

Sheets v. Dziabis, 738 F. Supp. 307 (N.D. Ind. 1990)

Nasrullah was sometimes called the curmudgeon of the racetrack. He didn't like to leave his barn, he wouldn't break into a trot when he got to the track, and he was usually disruptive at the starting line. His jockey, Sir Gordon Richards, said he was "very, very difficult to ride." He was often called the Irish Rogue. But the Irish Rogue was a sire of champions.

He was originally bred by the Aga Khan. Prince Karim Aga Khan IV is the 49th Imam of Nizaris Ismailism and an international race horse owner. Nasrullah was a pretty good racehorse in England, but the Aga Khan did not want to keep the bad actor around his farm. Khan sold him to an Irish breeder, who soon found that Nasrullah's colts could run. Arthur "Bull" Hancock, of Claiborne Farms in the United States, bought the stallion for $340,000, a remarkable price, in 1949. America was in need of fresh bloodlines, and Nasrullah fit the bill. Hancock had the idea of selling ownership interests in the stallion to his friends. But this wouldn't be an ordinary partnership. Hancock's friends didn't want to invest for a profit; they had plenty of money of their own. Hancock's friends wanted to breed their valuable mares to the best stallions, and the only way they were going to do that with Nasrullah was to buy into the syndicate. So, Hancock sold 34 shares, or nominations, in Nasrullah. Each share entitled its owner to breed one mare per year to the stallion. That syndication was one of the most significant moments in United States horse-racing history. The addition of significant new European bloodlines into United States racehorses produced numerous champion racehorses including Bold Ruler, the sire of Secretariat. The new bloodlines were important, but so was the new format for the ownership of stallions.

As racehorses have become more valuable, putting their ownership out of the reach of the common person, or even the wealthy, many enterprising entrepreneurs have formed partnerships to own them. These partnerships, often called syndicates, own racing horses, broodmares, and most often breeding stallions. Syndicates (an unfortunate term, since it reminds one of criminal syndicates) typically have from 30 to 50 investors, with a general manager to make the executive decisions about the horse. A portion of the expenses of the horse are billed on a regular basis to the partners.

Successful racehorse stallions are usually retired to the breeding barn where they can hopefully produce colts and fillies who will also be champions. Owners of prized broodmares face a dilemma; will they buy a share of the horse to be syndicated and thus preserve a chance to breed to the new stallion, or not buy, save themselves a considerable investment, and lose the chance to breed to the stallion in the future? That is not an easy decision, but a breeder with valuable mares must buy in to protect their ability to produce well-bred colts.

The right to breed a mare is called a "season" or a "nomination." One of the primary legal questions about these stallion syndicates is whether they are "securities" under the state and federal securities laws. If they are "securities" then they must be registered, a time-consuming and expensive process, unless they have an exemption from the securities laws.

The Securities Act of 1933 defines a security as "any note, stock, treasury stock, security future, bond, or investment contract." Interests in horse-racing syndicates are most likely an investment contract if they are covered by the Securities Act. In *Sec. & Exch. Comm'n v. W. J. Howey*, 328 U.S. 293 (1946), the United States Supreme Court defined an "investment contract" as "a contract, transaction or scheme whereby a person invests his money in a common enterprise and is led to expect profits solely from the efforts of the promoter or a third party."

Gainesway Farms is one of the legendary breeding farms in history. The original Kentucky Derby winner, Aristide, is buried there. John Gaines, the farm's founder, wanted to syndicate a stallion but wasn't sure whether the deal would be covered by the securities laws. Gaines asked for a no-action letter from the SEC. The SEC agreed that it would take no action against Gaines if:

1. The costs of the syndicate would be paid pro rata in proportion to the number of nominations each owner was entitled to use.
2. If, at the end of the first breeding season, the agreed-upon fertility of the stallion was not achieved, a breeder-owner could rescind the transaction.
3. The stallion would stand at Gainesway Farm with either Mr. Gaines or Gainesway acting as agent for the owners in performing custodial functions, but the stallion could be moved and the custodian changed upon vote of an agreed-upon percentage of the owners.
4. The compensation to the agent (Gainesway Farms) would be the right to use an agreed-upon number of nominations each breeding season.

5. Excess nominations would be given to certain of the breeder-owners determined through a drawing by lot.
6. Each owner would have an insurable interest in the stallion.
7. An owner could sell his or her fractional interest only after extending a right of first refusal to the other owners.
8. An owner could sell any nomination he or she did not use to another breeder, which need not be a breeder-owner.

This Gainesway no-action letter is one of the principal documents interpreting the *Howey* case in the horse-racing context. But the SEC is not the only potential complainant in stallion syndication.

Two investors in a stallion syndication of Bonnie Brae Farms went to court claiming securities fraud because Bonnie Brae Farms had told them that they could sell their nominations to other breeders at a net profit with no risk of loss. The first question was whether the federal and state securities laws would apply, that is, whether the stallion syndication was a security. The court didn't think so. The court didn't think this was a "common venture" under the *Howey* test. The fortunes of the various owners were not tied to the success of the venture. Since each investor was purchasing a nomination, which would primarily depend for its success on the investor's mare that bore the colt, and on the care and training of the horse, the success of the venture for each individual owner did not rely on the overall success of the syndicate. A rising tide did not float all boats equally. The syndicate was designed for the use or consumption of the item purchased, not to derive profit from the overall venture. Accordingly, the investment was not covered by the securities law, according to the court. But fairly subtle differences make a big difference in this field.

International Bloodstock Agency was syndicating two stallions, Aly North and Speedy Nijinsky. Each stallion was divided into 40 parts or seasons and sold to the public. Stephen Sheets was interested in the shares but he did not own any mares. Dr. Marvin Dziabis told Sheets that limited partnerships had been formed to purchase mares to breed to the stallions. The owners of the stallion shares would have the first right to sell their seasons to the limited partnerships for the price stated in a letter they would receive when they purchased the stallion shares. Dr. Dziabis said that the stallion shares were a good investment since there would be almost a 100 percent return on that money. Somehow, it didn't work out, and Sheets sued, claiming the stallion shares were securities under the Securities Act. And the court agreed.

The court said that the syndicate agreement alone was not a security, but when the syndicate is combined with the limited partnerships to purchase the breeding seasons at an assured price, the two instruments must be considered as a whole. Since Sheets was relying on the syndicator's success in forming the limited partnerships, the partnerships were a security. In the Bonnie Brae Farms investment, selling the seasons or nominations was the responsibility of the individual syndicate owners, but with International Bloodstock, selling the syndicate interests was the responsibility of the syndicators. This fairly subtle difference was enough to make the stallion seasons, with the right to sell to the limited partnerships, a security covered by the securities laws.

Partnerships formed to race horses rather than to breed them are usually securities. People invest in racing partnerships primarily for the thrill of the game but also for the slight chance that they will own one of the extraordinary horses that bring their owners fame and fortune. Money is invested, usually in limited liability companies being managed by the sellers, in the hopes that the horse will do well and float all boats. This is a classic investment where money is invested in a common venture, premised on an expectation of a return, from the efforts of the managers of the investment.

Chapter 12

Misrepresentation

A horse is a horse, of course, of course, that is, of course, unless the horse is . . . a gelding. In the world of horse racing, the term "horse" can have several different meanings. To laypeople, it is used to refer to any or all of the equine competitors on the racetrack. But to those familiar with the racing industry, it has a much more specific meaning. Within the business, the term "horse" refers to a male animal who has reached breeding age and who has not been castrated. The terms "stallion" or "stud" may also be used to denote the same thing. Conversely, "gelding" refers to a male horse that has been castrated.

In 1962, an animal named Cur-Non was entered to race in the Fonner Park Purse, a claiming race at Sunland Park Race Track in Sunland Park, New Mexico, just outside of El Paso, Texas. A claiming race is like a horse-racing garage sale, in that every horse in the race is for sale. Anyone who wishes to purchase one of the horses in the race may enter a "claim" immediately prior to the race, and thereby purchase the animal. In this particular race, the selling price was $3,500. However, claiming an animal from one of these races comes with significant risk. The potential owner often has no opportunity to inspect the animal prior to the race. Typically, the only chance to look the animal over is in the brief moments the animal appears in the saddling paddock prior to the race. If the claim is entered, that is, if the purchase is made, the animal becomes the property of the new owner the moment it crosses the finish line. In fact, the new owner must be ready to take possession of the animal before it leaves the track. It is a common occurrence to see a claimed animal pull up after the race, the former owner pull the saddle and bridle off, and the new owner slip on the halter and take possession.

Henry and Kathryn Grandi, a husband and wife, were interested in purchasing Cur-Non from the Fonner Park Purse. They were looking for a stallion to use in their own equine-breeding operation, and Cur-Non seemed to be just the animal they were looking for. Understanding the risks, they did everything within their power to inspect Cur-Non prior to the race. They surveyed him in the paddock and felt confident. More importantly, they inspected his entry in the racing program, which, in listing the sex of the animal, specifically designated Cur-Non as a "horse." Relying on the racing program's confirmation that the animal was, in fact, capable of breeding, the Grandis entered their claim and, following the race, took possession of Cur-Non.

Cur-Non was not, in fact, a horse. He was a gelding. Born in Kentucky in 1957, he had been registered later that year with the Jockey Club, the organization that oversees thoroughbred breeding and issues registration papers for each animal. These registration papers are necessary to enter any thoroughbred into a race anywhere in the United States. At the time Cur-Non's papers were issued, he was still fully intact.

However, the following year, Cur-Non was sold to R.S. LeSage, who promptly shipped the animal to Golden Gate Park, in

San Francisco, where, under the orders of LeSage, Cur-Non was castrated. The trouble was, LeSage never bothered to notify the Jockey Club that he had castrated Cur-Non, nor did he have new registration papers issued to reflect the change.

In the ensuing years, LeSage began to race Cur-Non. Then, in 1961, LeSage hired race trainer H.R. Claggett to take over Cur-Non's training, and the horse was immediately shipped to Sunland Park. There, at the direction of LeSage, Claggett continued to enter and race Cur-Non using the old racing papers that showed the animal to be a "horse," and the racetrack, not knowing otherwise, continued to publish that information in its racing program.

Following the January 6, 1962, race in which the Grandis claimed Cur-Non, they took possession and soon noticed the anatomical inaccuracy. Upon realizing that an important part of their "horse" was missing, they contacted LeSage by letter and let him know of their displeasure. They offered to return the animal in exchange for a full refund of the $3,500 claiming price, but received no response. Next, they sought out LeSage at the Sunland Park racetrack, again informing him of the situation. LeSage took the offer under advisement but soon told the Grandis that he was not liable for the problem and refused their offer.

Understandably upset, the Grandis filed a lawsuit against LeSage and the former trainer, Claggett, alleging that the two had misrepresented Cur-Non's physical condition. The trial court ultimately ordered that the Grandis were entitled to return Cur-Non to LeSage and to receive a refund, which they could collect from either LeSage or Claggett. It was also ordered that the Grandis were entitled to collect money from LeSage or Claggett for the costs they had incurred in feeding and keeping the Cur-Non since the date of the race. Naturally, LeSage and Claggett appealed.

The case wound its way through the New Mexico court system, ultimately arriving in the Supreme Court of New Mexico. After reviewing the case, the court essentially agreed with the trial court. They determined that, because LeSage had been well aware of Cur-Non's "condition," and because he had continued to race the animal in that condition under false pretenses, he had misrepresented the animal to potential buyers, including the Grandis. However, the court did take some sympathy on Claggett, finding that, although he had undoubtedly known that Cur-Non was a gelding, he had not personally profited from the misrepresentation in any way. As such, the Grandis could not hold him personally accountable, and could not collect their refund directly from him.

Misrepresentation May Be Unintentional

Although the court's decision in *Grandi v. LeSage* made clear that when an owner intentionally misrepresents the sex of an animal in a claiming race, the duped buyer is entitled to return the horse, other courts have clarified that even when the misrepresentation was accidental, the unfortunate buyer may still have an opportunity to correct the mistake.

In a case very similar to that of *Grandi v. LeSage*, Alvin Brodsky, a licensed thoroughbred owner in New York, claimed a horse from a race at Aqueduct Racetrack in New York City. As in *Grandi*, the horse in question had been listed in the track's racing program, as well as in the "affidavit of ownership" delivered to Brodsky following his claim, as a "colt," meaning that the animal was a noncastrated male that was three years old or younger. However, apparently realizing the mistake, John Nerud, the seller of the horse who had entered the claiming race, informed the New York Racing Association (NYRA), which operated the racetrack, of the problem prior to the race's start. To correct the issue, NYRA made an announcement over the track's public address system.

Despite the announcement, Brodsky claimed he never realized the actual sex of the animal until after he took possession. Realizing the mistake, Brodsky contacted the NYRA stewards, and asked for them to rescind the sale. They refused, and Brodsky brought suit.

The trial court initially denied Brodsky's claims, asserting that he had received sufficient notice of the condition. However, upon appeal, the Appellate Division of the New York Court determined that, although Nerud's actions were not intentional, they were potentially negligent, and it allowed Brodsky's claim to continue.

Chapter 13

Is Interference on the Racetrack a Tort?

Youst v. Longo, 729 P.2d 728 (Cal. 1987)

Harlan Youst was optimistic about the chances of Bat Champ, his horse, in the $100,000 eighth race at Hollywood Park. But Gerald Longo drove his horse, The Thrilly Brudder, into the path of Bat Champ, and then hit Bat Champ with a whip. Bat Champ broke stride, slowed down, and finished a miserable sixth (out of the money) in the race. Youst promptly filed a protest with the track judges, who agreed with his complaint, and The Thrilly Brudder, who had finished in front, was disqualified. As a result of The Thrilly Brudder's disqualification, Bat Champ was moved up to fifth in the race, entitling him to $5,000. But Youst thought that Bat Champ could have won the race ($50,000), or finished much better, if he had not been interfered with. Since he was so clearly wronged and the track judges had agreed, Youst wanted more; he wanted his actual loss as he saw it. So Youst filed suit in court to recover his losses, just like auto accident victims file suit in court to recover their losses. But therein lies the issue; is Youst's expectation that he would have finished better than fifth in a horse race something that should be compensated in court, just like the loss of a leg or arm? The courts have long been willing to protect reasonable economic expectancy against improper interference. Thus, an employer may have a cause of action against someone who talks his or her employee into quitting in violation of the contract of employment. An auto driver whose arm is broken by a negligent driver can sue and recover the wages the driver thinks he would have made but for the accident. But can a horse owner who thinks his horse is going to win a horse race sue for the loss in earnings caused by wrongful interference? The California Supreme Court said no. It doesn't make any difference whether the horse was 20 lengths ahead or just a nose ahead when it was interfered with, a horse owner or anyone in an athletic contest cannot sue for the anticipated loss. This was a fine line the court was drawing. The courts have protected all sorts of expectations against interference. The expectation that someone will perform under an established contract or will even enter into a contract has been protected. But the expectation that someone is going to finish well in a horse race or sporting contest, no matter how reasonable that expectation is, will not be protected in a court in California. Other states, following the Restatement of Torts, are more generous in finding a legal cause of action. Most of them are willing to find a cause of action if the chances of winning or finishing better are substantial.

Youst might have won the eighth race at Hollywood if Longo had not interfered; he may believe that he would have won. And if he had won, he would have made $50,000, but instead he made $5,000. Longo's interference possibly cost him $45,000 but he had no remedy in court, not even a chance to prove his case before a jury.

Chapter 14

Promising Again

McDevitt v. Stokes, 174 Ky. 515 (1917)

Certain cases are textbook favorites; *McDevitt v. Stokes* is one of them. The simple facts of this 1917 Kentucky case, involving some of the outstanding horses of the day, fit nicely into a controversial legal doctrine.

Mike McDevitt was one of the best harness drivers of turn-of-the-century America. He was described as a driver of "skill and experience" by the court. Captain David Shaw retained McDevitt to drive his horse, Grace, a "horse of great promise," in the Kentucky Futurity.

The Kentucky Futurity is a stakes race for three-year-old trotters, held each year at the Lexington, Kentucky, Red Mile. A prestigious race, it is one leg of the trotting Triple Crown. Winning the Kentucky Futurity was not only a great accomplishment for the winner, but also of great benefit to the winning horse's sire and dam. All of the horses related to the Kentucky Futurity winner became more valuable in the sale barn as buyers tried to find another Kentucky Futurity winner. The race even paid a small part of the purse to the owners of the dam of the winner. So, the owner of Grace's dam, and of many of her brothers and sisters, W. E. B. Stokes, also had great personal interest in Grace's performance in the race. Grace was the daughter of Peter the Great, one of the foundation sires of harness racing. He was a little-known horse from Kalamazoo, Michigan, when as a two-year-old he finished second in the Kentucky Futurity. He came back the next year to win the Kentucky Futurity. Stokes bought him at a sale in Madison Square Garden. Although Peter the Great was a fast horse, his legacy is not on the track, but from the over 500 horses he sired. There is a monument to Peter the Great on the Western Michigan University campus in Kalamazoo where he was born.

The Red Mile is located in the City of Lexington, Kentucky. It is the iconic track of harness racing. Founded in 1875, the one-mile oval (unusual in harness racing, where half mile tracks are more common) is made of red clay, hence the name of the track. That one mile of red clay has produced some of the fastest times in harness racing. Horsemen bring their fast horses to the Red Mile to establish a record speed for that horse. The track has the only round barn in horse racing.

Even though McDevitt was legally obligated to drive Grace and use his best efforts to win the race, Stokes, the owner of the mother, brothers, and sisters of Grace, offered to pay McDevitt an additional $1,000 if Grace won the race. Stokes had much to gain in the Kentucky Futurity also.

Grace won the race and Stokes refused to pay McDevitt. When McDevitt sued to collect on the promise to him, Stokes said that there was not an enforceable contract since there was no consideration for his promise. McDevitt was already obligated to drive Grace and make every effort to win the race in his legally binding contract with Grace's owner, Captain Shaw. Stokes argued that although he did promise to pay McDevitt, McDevitt did not promise anything in return to him other than a performance that he was already legally obligated to perform. Stokes argued that there was no consideration for his promise and, thus, it was not legally enforceable.

The Kentucky Court of Appeals (the highest appellate court in Kentucky at the time) agreed with Stokes; there was no consideration for the contract. *McDevitt could not recover the money promised him.* Courts have long felt that these promises, when there is already an existing enforceable obligation, run the risk of extortion; that is, why would any third party (Stokes) ever agree to pay when there is already an existing legal obligation (by McDevitt), unless the person promising to perform has threatened to breach his legal contract?

This has turned out to be a controversial area of the law. Not all courts are in agreement with this doctrine. The more the facts suggest an illegal refusal to perform a duty, the more likely the courts will not enforce the new promise. On the other hand, when there is no suggestion of illegal coercion, but rather a genuine desire to give someone an additional incentive to perform an important contract, as in this horse-racing case, the courts are now more willing to enforce the promise.

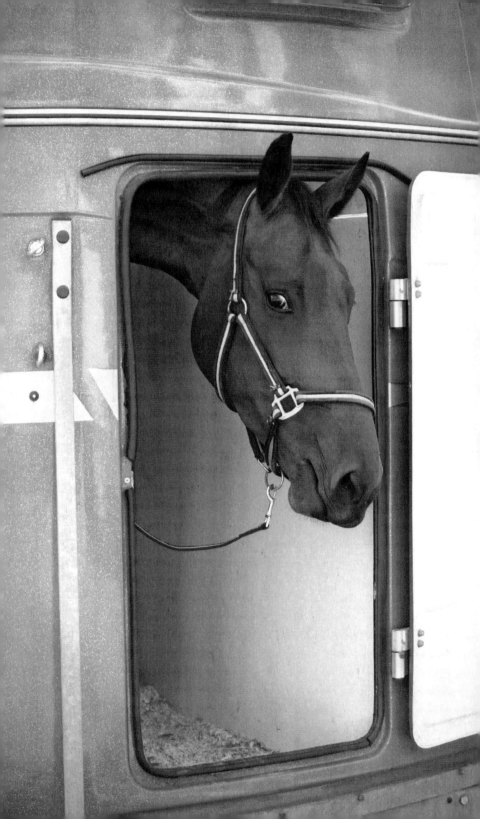

Chapter 15

The Mystery of Shergar

O'Brien & Others v. Hughes-Gibb & Co. Ltd., Chancery Div. (1995) L.R.L.R. 90 (Justice Rattee)

Shergar was the European Horse of the Year in 1981. He won the Epsom Derby by the greatest distance in history. He was an equine superstar.

Shergar was owned by Prince Karim Aga Khan IV, an international businessman, racehorse owner, and 49th Imam of Nizari Ismailism. The Nizari Ismails are a denomination of the Shia Muslims with between 5 million and 15 million followers who tithe regularly. The Aga Khan IV is believed to be one of the ten richest royals in the world, even though he has no geographic area to govern. He lives in Gouviex, France, on a large estate, but Shergar was born and raised on the Aga Khan's estate in the Irish horse country.

After winning his first races in a convincing manner, Shergar was the odds-on favorite to win the Epsom Derby, England's most prestigious race. Shergar was ridden in the Derby by a 19-year-old jockey, Walter Swinburn, who was riding in his first Derby. When the race began, Swinburn wisely let the horse run, putting his hands down on the horse's shoulders. He won by such a distance that the trailing horse's jockey thought that he had won the

Derby, only to discover another horse in front of him. Shergar next raced in the Irish Derby, where he easily won by 4 lengths. Shergar was an Irish national hero. He was syndicated in 1983 in anticipation of his breeding career. Thirty-four shares of the horse were sold for £250,000 each (approximately $453,650 in American dollars), while the Aga Khan kept six shares for himself. The sale established Shergar's value at approximately $18 million dollars, a record valuation at that time. After his sale, Shergar raced his only poor race, finishing an anemic fourth in the St. Leger Stakes at Dorcaster. After that, he was retired to stud, having won six out of his lifetime eight races.

In October of 1981 Shergar went back to the Irish horse country. He was greeted by the town band and schoolchildren waving flags of his racing colors in the town of Newbridge. The Aga Khan, then a minority owner, was there to greet the triumphant hero.

Shergar was stabled at Ballymany Stud in the Irish horse country. Since there had never been a horse theft in that area before, the farm had little security. Shergar bred 35 mares his first season (1982) for a stud fee of £80,000 each (approximately $174,000 at the time).

On the evening of February 8, 1983, a horse trailer pulled into the area where Shergar was being stabled, just off the main Dublin road. Shergar's caretaker, Jim Fitzgerald, lived nearby and thought that he heard a car in the yard but forgot about it when nothing more happened. Then there was a knock on Fitzgerald's door. Fitzgerald's son answered the door, turned around to summon his father, and was struck in the small of his back, knocking him to the floor. Several men, one with a machine-gun, pushed their way into the house and held the Fitzgerald family at gunpoint. Shergar was going to be kidnapped. (Other horses are stolen; Shergar was kidnapped.)

The thieves forced Jim Fitzgerald to go with them to the barn where Shergar was stabled, and to help load the horse into their horse trailer. Shergar was hauled away, and Jim Fitzgerald was taken in another vehicle, driven around for several hours, and then released near where he lived. The thieves picked a good day for driving away with the horse trailer; it was the day of the major horse sale in Ireland and many horse trailers were on the road.

The investigation and search for Shergar went badly. Fitzgerald got in touch with the farm manager, who called the horse's vet, who called the Irish Finance Minister, who called the Irish Minister of Justice, who summoned the police, the Gardi, eight hours after Fitzgerald's first call.

Shergar was not an easy horse to hide. He was a standard bay but he had a distinct white patch on his face. Given the massive publicity that accompanied his racing career and theft, there was little chance that Shergar was going to be sold to a legitimate buyer. His value to thieves was in a demand of ransom from one of the richest men in the world, the Aga Khan IV. If only the richest man owned him.

The investigation of the theft was headed by Detective James Spud Murphy. Murphy added a great deal of color to the investigation with his distinct trilby hat, his consultation with psychics about the whereabouts of the horse, and his response to a reporter's question, "A clue . . . that is what we don't have." Farms and stables across Ireland were searched in vain.

Shergar was a relatively young and vigorous male horse. He was used to daily exercise with his caretaker, Jim Fitzgerald. There is no doubt that the thieves would have a difficult task taking care of such a horse.

The famous horse-race author, Dick Francis, had written the book, *Blood Sport*, which described the theft of a well-known fictional stallion. "I hope the thief did not get their idea from me," said Francis.

What followed was farce. Many kidnappers called with their demands. The racing reporter for *The Sun* received a telephone call instructing him to go to a hotel in Belfast to await instructions on paying a ransom for Shergar. Two other reporters received the same message. With great fanfare, they flew to Belfast to await word. Television cameras and newsmen packed the lobby of the hotel when the phone call came in. All of Ireland listened to the call. The reporters were told to proceed to a farm about 30 miles north, where further instructions would be forthcoming. When the reporters went to the farm to await instructions, they received one call asking for a reduced ransom and then, in another call, were told that Shergar was dead. These calls were almost certainly a hoax. In May of 1983, the police called off the searches for Shergar.

Shergar was owned by 24 different owners, each of whom was responsible for insurance. Consequently, there were many different kinds of insurance on the horse. The owners whose insurance policies covered theft were successful in collecting under their policies. Lloyd's of London announced that it had paid over $10.5 million on the theft of Shergar. But many other insurance companies that had policies covering the death of the horse refused to pay until his death was proven. Without Shergar's body, that would be difficult.

Coolmore Stud, the largest thoroughbred breeding operation in the world, had three shares of Shergar. Its insurance policy covered only the death of the horse. The insurance company refused to pay the £200,000 due under the policy for the death of the horse. Coolmore sued its insurers in London's High Court, contending that the insurers were negligent in failing to provide insurance that covered the theft of their horse. But the London judge thought that horse theft in Ireland was a rare event so it was understandable that the insurance policy didn't cover it.

No one knows what happened to Shergar. There are two prominent theories of what happened. One is that the IRA took the horse for ransom. Sean O'Callaghan, an IRA member serving a life sentence for two murders, told the *London Sunday Times* that Shergar was alive for only a few hours after his theft. O'Callaghan said that Shergar was taken by the IRA for ransom to purchase newer and better weapons but the deal went bad when the horse became uncontrollable and had to be shot and buried in a wood. There are doubts about this theory. O'Callaghan was a criminal who was not believable or trustworthy and the IRA usually claimed responsibility for its misdeeds, which it had not done in this case.

The other prominent theory is that Colonel Muammar el-Quaddafi took Shergar. Quaddafi hated the Aga Khan. Quaddafi was ruthless enough to do it and had the money and resources to carry it out. But it is doubtful that foreign terrorists could pull off such an operation in Ireland. So we will always be left to wonder about the mystery of Shergar.

Chapter 16

Torts

On July 13, 1978, jockey Ron Turcotte swung his leg over the back of a four-year-old mare named Flag of Leyte Gulf at the Belmont Park racecourse in Queens, New York. Although still two weeks shy of his 37th birthday, Turcotte had already ridden in more than 20,000 thoroughbred races as a jockey, and had won more than 3,000. Of French-Canadian descent, Turcotte had risen to fame in the 1960s and 1970s, most notably for his Triple Crown–winning campaign aboard the copper-red thunderbolt known as Secretariat.

But despite his fame, Turcotte, like many of the well-known jockeys of the day, could not afford to ride only in the major races. He needed to earn a living, and there were not enough big races for a jockey to limit his career to the nation's major races. To make ends meet, virtually all jockeys, including Turcotte, had to ride in the rough-and-tumble daily races for minimum pay. And so it was that Turcotte found himself riding in this cheap race on a Thursday afternoon in July.

Turcotte and his mount were assigned to post-position three, meaning that he would start from the third spot out from the inside rail. In post-position two, immediately to his left, was jockey Jeffrey Fell, on a horse named Small Raja. To the outside, in post-position four, was a horse named Walter Malone. Then, in the mad confusion that is the start of every thoroughbred horse race, the gates flung open, the horses jostled against each other, and Turcotte's mount, Flag of Leyte Gulf, clipped heels with Walter Malone, in the process unseating Turcotte and violently hurling him to the ground. The impact was catastrophic, rendering Turcotte, one of racing's greatest stars, a paraplegic.

Turcotte subsequently brought a lawsuit to recover compensation for his injuries. The case presented several questions about the fundamental principles of the law of torts. Within the law, a tort is a legal principle that seeks to hold a person responsible when he or she intentionally or negligently causes another person to suffer harm. To prove that someone has acted negligently, as Turcotte would be required to do in his case, the plaintiff must prove three elements: (1) that the defendant owed the plaintiff a legal duty to act or refrain from acting in a certain way, (2) that the defendant breached or failed to comply with that duty, and (3) that the defendant's failure to comply with that duty caused the plaintiff to suffer harm. A common example of this negligence occurs when a defendant runs a traffic stop sign, crashes into the plaintiff, and causes the plaintiff to suffer injury. The defendant is negligent because the defendant owed the plaintiff a legal duty to not run the stop sign and to comply with the applicable traffic laws, the defendant breached that duty by failing to stop at the stop sign, and the defendant caused the plaintiff harm by crashing into him.

Turcotte brought his suit against the rider of the horse to his inside, Jeffrey Fell, as well as the horse's owner, David Reynolds, and the New York Racing Association (NYRA), the governing body of thoroughbred racing in New York, which owned and operated the Belmont Park Racetrack. Turcotte's complaint alleged that

Fell had a duty to comply with the rules and regulations of thoroughbred racing, that he breached that duty when he engaged in reckless, or "foul," riding, and that his recklessness had unreasonably caused Turcotte's horse to clip heels with the third horse, Walter Malone. Turcotte's complaint further alleged that, as the owner of the horse piloted by Fell, David Reynolds was responsible for both the horse and Fell's actions on the racetrack, under a legal doctrine known as respondeat superior. Further, the complaint alleged that NYRA was negligent because it had improperly maintained the racetrack, which caused the track to be unsafe, and which ultimately contributed to the accident by causing an unsafe racing surface.

After several years of legal wrangling, the case reached the Court of Appeals of New York, that state's highest court, in 1986. In hearing the case, the court was asked to address two basic legal questions. First, the court was asked to consider exactly what duty of care was owed by the defendants to Turcotte. The second question was much more nuanced and asked the court to determine whether Turcotte had assumed the risk of injury by riding in the race to begin with, given the fact that Turcotte's years of experience as a jockey made him aware that thoroughbred racing was an inherently dangerous activity, and if so, whether the accident in question, and Turcotte's subsequent injuries, where within the scope of the risk Turcotte had assumed by participating in the race.

In taking up these questions in Turcotte's case, the court evaluated them simultaneously. It recognized that all plaintiffs, including Turcotte, are entitled to certain legal protections from a defendant's negligent or reckless behavior. At the same time, it also recognized that Turcotte had undoubtedly been well aware of the dangers of his occupation. Thus, it immediately turned and ultimately hinged its decision upon a third factor by asking what risks, exactly, Turcotte had assumed.

In addressing this third question, the court ruled that when an individual, such as a jockey, assumes the risk of an inherently dangerous activity, he or she assumes only those risks that are naturally apparent. In other words, if a reasonable person evaluated the dangerous activity and determined the types of consequences that might naturally happen from engaging in that activity, then he or she has assumed the risks of injury if one of those apparent dangers does in fact cause the harm. Conversely, if the danger is somehow hidden, then the individual has not assumed the risk, because it is not the type of harm that the individual could have reasonably contemplated when he or she chose to engage in that dangerous activity. For example, it is unlikely that an individual would anticipate intentional or reckless conduct from another participant, and thus, if another participant does engage in such intentional or reckless activity, and that intentional or reckless activity is what actually causes the harm, then the conduct falls outside of that which the injured individual has consented to, and the participant who caused the harm may be held legally responsible for his or her conduct.

To determine the answer to this final question, that is, whether Turcotte assumed the risks of thoroughbred racing, and more specifically, whether the activity that Turcotte accused Jeffrey Fell of engaging in was within the scope of the activity to which Turcotte consented, the court examined the basics of thoroughbred racing. In this regard, it examined testimony that Turcotte himself had given under oath during the early stages of the case, in which he stated that the average thoroughbred weighs approximately 1,000 pounds, and runs at a speed of 40 miles per hour or more. He further testified that the average jockey weighs between 100 and 120 pounds, and that virtually every professional jockey had, at some point in his career, ridden horses that proved impossible to control. In fact, Turcotte had testified that many horses refused to run in a straight line, preferring instead to swerve back and forth across the track, often bumping into each other in the process.

Further, the court examined the rules governing race riding in New York, which Turcotte had alleged jockey Fell violated. It found that, although these rules were designed to promote safety among both the horses and jockeys, they were, at times, impossible to comply with, given the independent nature of the horses themselves.

Ultimately, the court determined that the actions of jockey Fell, and the resulting consequences, including Turcotte's paralysis, were within the scope of activity that Turcotte had consented to when he chose to participate in that fateful race, and it found in favor of jockey Fell. For the same reason, it dismissed Turcotte's case against David Reynolds, the owner of the horse jockey Fell was riding. For similar reasons, it also dismissed the case against NYRA, finding that Turcotte had assumed the risk of riding on the track, given that he was well experienced with not only racetrack maintenance in general, but the conditions of the Belmont track in particular.

Despite the tragic results of his injury, Turcotte remained active in the horse-racing industry. He became a supporter of the Permanently Disabled Jockey Fund, which seeks to raise money for jockeys who have suffered catastrophic injuries on the track. He has been inducted into both the United States Thoroughbred Hall of Fame in Saratoga, New York, and the Canadian Racing Hall of Fame. In May of 2013, the National Film Board of Canada released a documentary film about his life, which is titled "Secretariat's Jockey, Ron Turcotte."

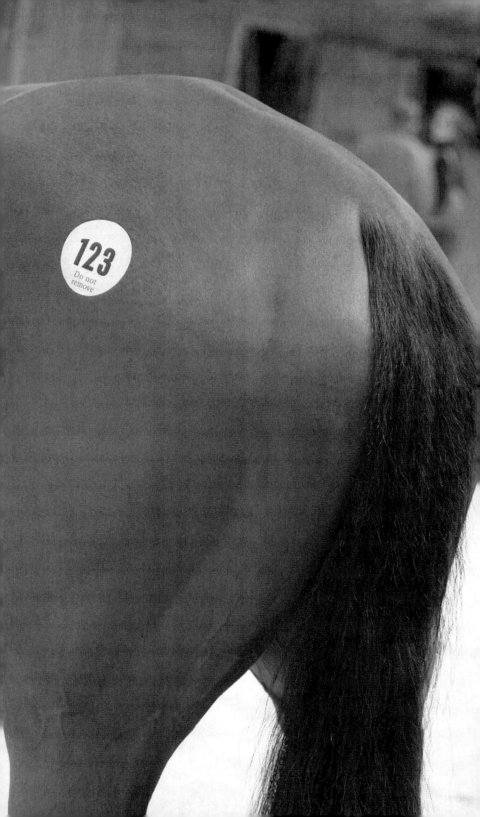

Chapter 17

Buying and Selling a Horse and How Not to Do It

Keeneland Ass'n, Inc. v. Eamer, 830 F. Supp. 974 (E.D. Ky. 1993)

Miron v. Yonkers Raceway, 400 F.2d 112 (C.A.N.Y. 1967)

One of the great duels of horse-racing history was the three races of the Triple Crown of 1978. Affirmed beat Alydar three times to win the Triple Crown by a combined two lengths. The final Triple Crown race, the Belmont, was an epic battle down the stretch between the two. Alydar has been called the greatest horse never to win a Triple Crown race. But Alydar had his revenge in the breeding shed, going on to establish himself as one of the great stallions of his time. He is now a member of horse racing's Hall of Fame.

Ray Stark had some prize broodmares and purchased two seasons to Alydar. Stark agreed to take the colt from one of the mares and share the colt from his prize mare, Careless Notion, with the breeder, Calumet Farms. Careless Notion had a broken knee, so she and her colt were kept separate from the other mares and colts. When the colt of Careless Notion was weaned from her mother, the filly was not used to being with other foals so she "ran the fence" looking for her mother. This habit wore her feet down and made her front feet sore. The filly was examined by a veterinarian, who placed fiberglass purple and green tape on her front hooves. The veterinarian had the colt x-rayed but found no serious faults with her feet. So, Careless Notion's colt was shipped to Kentucky for the upcoming yearling sale.

Calumet Farms, the partial owner of Careless Notion's filly, was fast approaching its end. Serious mismanagement had taken a heavy toll on Calumet Farms. Alydar died from a suspicious broken leg in his stall. The Calumet horses were being sold, and since Careless Notion's filly was partly owned by Calumet, she was shipped to Keeneland, one of the big sale barns in horse racing. At Keeneland, the horses were available for inspection long before the sale, and their medical records were kept at a repository of information nearby. Careless Notion's filly did not have her previous x-ray records from the farm with her, since the veterinarian thought they were of no interest to a buyer.

Richard Eamer, an experienced horse owner and lawyer, bid $350,000 for the filly. Immediately after the sale, another veterinarian found that the filly had substantial problems in her hind legs and also some dislocation of the front coffin bones. Eamer notified Keeneland that he was revoking his purchase. The filly was resold at a subsequent sale for $25,000. A $325,000 loss will bring about a lawsuit. Keeneland sued Eamer for the $350,000 purchase price.

The Uniform Commercial Code (UCC) is a set of laws governing commercial transactions in most states. Since horses are considered "goods" under the UCC, the UCC governs most horse sales. The UCC provides for express warranties for statements about the goods or horse, and the implied warranty of merchantability, which may be part of any sale of a horse.

Express Warranties

Express warranties include any affirmation of fact or description of a horse that becomes part of the deal. Express warranties may be either written or oral. A party does not even have to intend to make an express warranty to be bound by one. One of the major problems in horse racing is whether statements about a horse are representations of fact to be relied upon by the buyer or just the opinion or "puffing" of the seller. When the horse Red Carpet was entered in the "Old Glory Sale" at Yonkers Raceway, the bidding went to $17,000 when an agent of the seller took the microphone and said:

> He's as sound—as, as gutty a horse as you want to find anywhere. He'll race a good mile for you every time. He's got loads of heart and you're way off on the price of this horse.

Red Carpet went on to sell for $32,000. But, when the buyer tried to exercise the horse the next day, the heart was gone. Red Carpet limped badly on the track. But, was the statement about the "soundness" of the horse a warranty that was part of the basis of the bargain, or was it mere sales talk or puffing, things that no rational buyer would rely on, especially in the context of a racehorse sale? The court believed that the representations that the horse was sound were a warranty. The question at trial was whether the horse had developed lameness before or after the sale.

But there were no express warranties made in the sale of Careless Notion's filly at Keeneland. Eamer would have to look further for a law to support his attempted rescission of his purchase.

Implied Warranty of Merchantability

There are also certain warranties that are inherent in the sale process regardless of what the seller says. Sellers who hold themselves out as having knowledge or skill peculiar to the goods sold, here racehorses, or to whom such knowledge or skill may be attributed (e.g., experienced horsemen and trainers) are merchants, and when they sell horses, they make an implied warranty of merchantability. Any horseman who regularly sells racehorses is probably a merchant. In order to be merchantable, the goods or horse must be "fit for the ordinary purposes" for which those goods are used. Racehorses are purchased for racing and breeding, so they must be fit for those purposes. But in the horse-racing world, "fit for ordinary purposes" does not require the horse to win races or perform at superior levels but rather to perform as a racehorse. Eamer could certainly contend that he purchased Careless Notion's filly for $350,000 for the serious purpose of racing the filly. If the filly was not fit to race, then there was a breach of the implied warranty of merchantability.

But Was There a Warranty?

Most racehorse auction sales come with a sales catalog showing the breeding of each horse for sale, one horse per page. The catalogs also contain the conditions of sale, which are usually of little interest to the buyer who is dreaming of the winner's circle. The Keeneland Sale contained a condition of sale, which included:

THERE IS NO WARRANTY IMPLIED BY AUCTIONEER OR CONSIGNOR (INCLUDING OWNER), EXCEPT AS SET FORTH HEREIN, AS TO THE MERCHANTABILITY OR

FITNESS FOR ANY PARTICULAR PURPOSE OF ANY ANI-
MAL OFFERED IN THIS SALE. ALL SALES ARE MADE ON
AN AS IS BASIS, WITH ALL FAULTS. *(Emphasis in original)*

Chapter 18

Breakage

Under the pari-mutuel style of wagering, racetracks take the total amount wagered on a race, deduct a percentage for the track and the government (usually around 15 percent), and pay the rest back to the bettors by dividing the balance by the total number of winning tickets. But the tracks pay only on 10-cent increments; one would not see a $3.43 payout. The tracks always round the payouts down to the nearest 10-cent increment (sometimes to the nearest 20-cent increment), so the payout in the above example would be $3.40. The 3-cent difference between the calculated payout and the actual 10-cent payout is called the "breakage." Obviously, there is no way to tell ahead of time what the breakage will be on any particular wager but smart bettors know that the breakage affects different wagers differently. Since breakage will always be less than 10 cents, it is more significant for favorites where the payout will be smaller than it is for long shots where the payout is larger. Thus, the less-than-10-cent breakage on a $2.40 payout is much more significant than a less-than-10-cent breakage on a

$20 payout. Breakage is not very much money for the individual bettor but it is a lot of money for the tracks.

Horsemen's organizations, particularly the Horsemen's Benevolent and Protective Association (HBPA), often represent the horse owners in negotiating agreements with the track. Those agreements call for the track to pay a percentage of the handle (total amount bet) to the owners in the form of purses. Sometimes the percentage also includes the total breakage for the race meeting, which is a substantial amount of money.

Chapter 19

Cloning Horses

Abraham & Veneklasen Joint Venture v. Am. Quarter Horse Ass'n, 2013 WL 2297104 (N.D. Tex.)

I guess we all knew it was going to get here—cloning, that is. The old canard—one male, one female—just wasn't going to work anymore. It's going to be one female and, ah, let's see, someone else. Scientists have a way of ruining everything and as with most scientific advancements, the law must react to a new reality.

The reproductive process has always been a matter of controversy in the horse world and especially in the horse-racing world. The Jockey Club, which regulates thoroughbreds (runners), requires live cover (please don't ask for an explanation) to produce a foal that may be registered. The United States Trotting Association, which regulates standardbreds (harness horses), has allowed artificial insemination. But the big question confronting the horse industry today and horse racing in particular is cloning.

Cloning allows the breeder to produce a genetically identical offspring. In the cloning process the breeder takes an unfertilized egg and removes the nucleus. The nucleus is then replaced by a cell from a donor animal. The nucleus-egg combination is then given an electrochemical stimulus, which fuses the two and produces a clone embryo. That embryo then begins to naturally divide. The embryo is then implanted into a host mother to raise the embryo in the normal gestation process.

Horsemen are concerned about producing a genetically identical offspring. If you could produce a genetically identical offspring of Secretariat or Animal Kingdom, why fool around with the mystery of the live cover breeding process, which is so unpredictable?

Problems arise when the horsemen band together in nonprofit organizations to regulate their industry. The American Quarter Horse Association (AQHA) has approximately 281,000 members who are breeders, trainers, and racers. The AQHA registers quarter horses, and only the AQHA-registered horses are eligible to compete in numerous AQHA-sanctioned quarter horse shows and races. The AQHA has a Stud Book Registration Committee of 25 to 35 members who make recommendations to the board on registration rules. The Stud Book Registration Committee is comprised of elite horse breeders, who are often competitors of the upstart cloners. The committee recommended and the board adopted rules that barred cloned horses from registration.

The first animal to be successfully cloned was Dolly the sheep, who was cloned in Scotland by the Roslin Institute in 1996. The technology moved slowly westward so that a horse was cloned at Texas A&M in 2005. Dr. Gregg Veneklasen, a Texas veterinarian, became interested in cloning and began tinkering with the technology shortly after it arrived in the United States. Veneklasen was none too happy about the ban on registration of quarter horses by the AQHA. Dr. Veneklasen was charging over $150,000 per foal, but if the result of his cloning couldn't race or enter the aqha horse shows, the demand for his services would suffer. He did what all good Americans do in that situation—he sued somebody.

Section 1 of the Sherman Act provides:

Every contract, combination in the form of trust or otherwise, or conspiracy, in restraint of trade or commerce among the several States, or with foreign nations, is declared to be illegal.

But the courts have held that they didn't mean *every* contract. (So much for the strict constructionists.) What the Congress really meant, according to the courts, is that all contracts that unreasonably restrain competition are illegal. But the Act requires in Section 1 that there be a contract—that is, that there be two parties in agreement. The AQHA, by itself, is not a contract, combination, or conspiracy. But viewed another way, as the court did in Dr. Veneklasen's case, the AQHA is made up of breeders, owners, and trainers who are working together in the form of the AQHA. Thus, if the AQHA unreasonably restrains trade by banning cloned horses, it violates the Sherman Act and Dr. Veneklasen has a cause of action.

Section 2 of the Sherman Act provides:

Every person who shall monopolize, or attempt to monopolize, or combine or conspire with any other person or persons, to monopolize any part of the trade or commerce among the several States, or with foreign nations, shall be deemed guilty of a felony.

Once again, the courts said they didn't really mean that every monopoly is prohibited. Sometimes businesses monopolize a field by providing better services or furnishing a better product. That's not prohibited even though the Act may say it is. What is prohibited is the possession of monopoly power and "the willful acquisition or maintenance of that power," as distinguished from providing a superior product or service. The AQHA certainly possesses monopoly power but the question was whether it willfully was acquiring or maintaining a monopoly by its actions regarding cloning. Since monopoly power is the power to exclude competition and the AQHA was certainly excluding competition from cloned horses, the court believed that a jury could find an antitrust violation.

On July 30, 2013, a federal court jury found that the AQHA had violated state and federal antitrust laws in excluding cloned horses from competition. The jury did not award any money damages to Dr. Veneklasen but the court has ordered the AQHA to register cloned quarter horses. The AQHA has appealed. While the jury's decision is not precedent, many will pay attention to it.

Australia has recently weighed in on the subject. Bruce McHugh, the former chairman of the Sydney Turf Club, challenged the ban on artificial insemination of thoroughbreds on grounds of antitrust (the Aussies call it, perhaps more correctly, competition law). But the Australian Court in a 375-page decision rejected the challenge, saying that the rule was reasonable since it had been in existence for many decades to prevent the attribution of incorrect paternity and the ban was also present in the International Studbook Committee. If Australian horses were bred by artificial insemination they would run the risk of being unable to race in international races.

The controversy over cloning and the artificial insemination of racehorses is not going away soon but new technology has a way of winning the day.

Chapter 20

Race Conditions; What Can Go Wrong?

Fattorusso v. Urbanowicz, 774 N.Y.S.2d 658 (2004)

Helad Farms v. Pennsylvania State Harness Racing Comm'n, 470 A.2d 181 (Pa. Cmwlth. 1984)

Each horse race has a condition for entry so that horses of equal speed and promise are racing each other. The racing secretary at the track is the person in charge of establishing the conditions of each race, assigning weights to be carried in thoroughbred races, and setting the purses for the race. The racing secretary tries to bring about a competitive race. If a horse is a prohibitive favorite, the bettors may be reluctant to wager on such an overwhelming favorite or conversely may be reluctant to wager on obvious long shots in the race. The track also runs the risk, if too many bet on the favorite, of having to pay a minimum required payout, which comes out of its pocket. There are a number of race conditions that the racing secretary may use.

Maiden Races

A race for nonwinners of a horse race is called a maiden race. Maidens may have won training races taking place before the pari-mutuel races but they haven't won a race for a purse during the betting program. When a maiden wins its first race, it "breaks its maiden" and is no longer eligible for maiden races. Some horses, sadly, race in the maiden races many times.

Allowance Races

A horse that has "broken his or her maiden" usually moves up to an allowance race. The allowance races have specific conditions for entry, for example, entrants must be nonwinners of three races in the current year. The conditions can become quite long and involved, for example, entrants must be fillies and mares three years old and upward that have not won four races or that have not won a race since December 16 of the previous year. Usually the conditions involve nonwinners of a certain number of races; nonwinners of a certain amount of money; horses that have not won a race since a certain date; or a combination of those conditions. Thoroughbred races often combine race conditions with weights to carry during the race to further handicap the race.

Claiming Races

In claiming races, every horse has a selling price that is set by the owner and is a condition of the race; for example, a condition of the race could be that every horse in the race may be purchased for $20,000. If you are a licensed horse owner and post the claiming price before the race, then the horse is yours after the race. There are lots of things that can go wrong in the claiming race process, especially when the buyer cannot inspect the horse before the race.

Louis Fattorusso claimed a horse at Yonkers Raceway that died of acute respiratory distress three days after the race. Fattorusso alleged that the respiratory distress was caused by the defendant seller negligently administering a "milkshake" just before the race. Horsemen illegally administer milkshakes by running a tube through the hose's nostrils into the horse's stomach and inserting baking soda and water. The baking soda is thought to neutralize the buildup of lactic acid in the horse's muscles so the horse will not tire as quickly during the race. Milkshaking can go awry when the person administering the milkshake misses the horse's stomach and puts the tube down the horse's windpipe and into the lungs. That's what Fattorusso alleged in this case— that the defendant put baking soda into the horse's lungs, causing the horse to eventually die. But the New York trial court judge was not impressed and dismissed the complaint.

The court ruled that the only grounds for setting a claim aside were set forth in the New York Racing Commission's regulations. The regulations said that the claim could be set aside for misrepresentations of age or gender, a positive test for equine anemia, an undisclosed pregnancy, an undisclosed nerve operation, or a postrace blood or urine sample that tests positive. None of these conditions were present in this case.

The plaintiff argued that the postrace urine samples did not test positive because the baking soda went down the wrong tube into the lungs rather than the stomach. The judge didn't care; there was no positive test for drugs so the claim could not be set aside.

Stakes Races

The most lucrative and prestigious races are the stakes races. Stake races usually require payments on a periodic basis over a period of time before the race. Many horses will make preliminary stakes payments even though only a few will enter. These unused, preliminary payments are added to the purse. Since many horses enter the best races and only a limited number end up racing or winning the race, these early payments contribute significantly to the race purses. The Kentucky Derby, the Preakness, and the Belmont are stakes races.

Many owners have several horses that require stakes payments to different races and different states at different times. Sometimes hundreds of different payments are required, which can be confusing. Consequently, services are available to make the required payments. One of those services is the Standardbred Stake Service of New York. In 1984 Standardbred sent the required payments for the Pennsylvania Sire Stakes before the May 15 due date. But the checks were facially defective and returned to Standardbred. Ralph Alfano, the administrator of the Pennsylvania Stake Fund, called the people at Standardbred and told them that since they had submitted their payment on time but defectively, he would give them more time to get their payment in to the fund. But Standardbred still did not submit its required stakes payment and the commission disqualified all of Standardbred's horses except eight horses owned by Lauxmont Farms. Lauxmont had found out about Standardbred's default, called Alfano, and sent its payments to the Stakes Fund, thus qualifying Lauxmont's horses but disqualifying the other 19 of Standardbred's horses owned by Standardbred's other owners. Standardbred eventually paid for the other 19 horses but the payment was almost a week late. Those checks were returned and the horses disqualified. So, all of Standardbred's horses were disqualified except for the Lauxmont Farms horses. That seemed unfair so the disqualified horse owners went to court.

After setting forth the grounds for reversing a racing commission order, the Pennsylvania court added one more. The court said, "It is sufficient that the complained-of conduct and its attending circumstances be such as to reflect negatively on the sport." That's a very subjective standard, not one that leads to an impartial objective analysis. Nevertheless, the Pennsylvania court thought that treating the different Standardbred Stake Service owners differently "reflected negatively on the sport" of harness racing and must be reversed. But instead of disqualifying all of the Standardbred Stake Service's horses for their late payment, the court ordered all of Standardbred Stake Service owners be given a chance to make their payments to qualify their horses.

Sire Stakes

For many years, future racing stars were born and bred on the bluegrass of Kentucky. They then went on to race at the big city tracks of New York, Los Angeles, and Chicago. But New York and other state breeders wanted part of the breeding and foaling operations in their state. Why should New York and California put on races for horses that were raised and foaled in another state? One answer is to use some of the money generated by the big, metropolitan tracks to sponsor big purse stakes races for horses bred in that state. Many of the states with major metropolitan tracks have done so with their state sire stakes. New York, New Jersey, Ohio, Indiana, Pennsylvania, California, Michigan, and Ontario have all established sire stakes in their states to promote their state breeding operations. But each time the rules of these stakes are

119

changed, someone gets hurt or loses an advantage and someone benefits, and that brings about lawsuits.

The New York Racing Commission changed the eligibility requirements for its lucrative final races by requiring horses to race at the smaller New York tracks like Batavia, Monticello, and Goshen and gain points to qualify for the higher-paying finals. Only the horses with the most qualifying points would be allowed into the finals. Two organizations representing harness horse breeders and racers sued. They claimed that the racing commission had no authority to change or establish the eligibility for the sire stakes. They argued that the legislature set up eligibility conditions when it said that only New York–bred horses could race in the New York Sire Stakes and, thereafter, the commission had no authority to change the legislation by establishing additional eligibility requirements. But the New York Supreme Court (the trial level court of general jurisdiction in New York) disagreed. The New York Supreme Court thought that since the applicable legislation excluded horses bred outside the state but did not necessarily include any horse, the commission was free, in its discretion, to condition entry into the sire stakes races. The sire stakes have had their desired effect. New York and the other states are developing major breeding farms, which are attractive because their foals will be eligible for the money-making state sire stakes.

Chapter 21

Horse-Racing Dates

In the horse-racing world, dates can be extremely important. The Kentucky Derby, for example, is always held at Churchill Downs on the first Saturday in May. The Preakness Stakes, the second leg of the Triple Crown, always follows two weeks later, and the Belmont Stakes, the third and final leg, occurs three weeks after that. Similarly, the races at Saratoga Race Course in Saratoga, New York, always take place later in the summer, giving rise to the nickname of the Travers Stakes, that track's feature race, as the "midsummer derby."

Although tradition certainly plays a role in determining when these races will be run at their respective tracks, there is another, more important factor that the tracks must take into account in determining when the operational dates of their racing meets will occur. That factor is money. Many states, including Kentucky, New York, and Michigan, have multiple racetracks, each seeking to host its own racing meets and thereby collect its own share of the gambling revenues. To eliminate the need for these tracks to compete against each other for horses, trainers, and jockeys, the racing commissions of each state typically allot specific "racing dates" to each track. In allotting racing dates, the commission will designate a time frame within which each track may operate its racing meet. Typically, the dates are allotted such that one track will have exclusive operation of all racing for a set period, and then, upon the conclusion of that mandated time, racing will move to another racecourse, which in turn gets its own exclusivity for several months.

The issue always lies in how these dates are allocated by the racing commission. The specific dates can have a drastic impact on the financial profits of a track. If the track is awarded dates during a time of the year that race fans are likely to attend the races, the track has a better chance of generating large profits. Conversely, if the track is allocated unfavorable racing dates, such as those in the dead of winter, the track's profits are likely to be small.

In some cases, the problem is solved by allocating the racing dates in accordance with how the population fluctuates within the state. For example, in New York, the dates are allocated to Aqueduct Racetrack in the winter and to Belmont Park in the spring. Both tracks are in the New York City borough of Queens, which keeps the racing action close to the major population center. Then, in the summer, when the population is more apt to be on vacation, the racing shifts to Saratoga Race Course in Saratoga, New York, which also happens to be a popular vacation destination.

Unfortunately, as you might imagine, when the allocation of racing dates can have a serious impact on a racetrack's profit, the battle over how those dates are awarded can become quite contentious. Nowhere has this been better illustrated, or more hotly contested, than in the racing date battles between two Miami, Florida, racetracks—Gulfstream Park and Hialeah Park.

Hialeah Park opened for racing in 1930 (it had actually opened for racing in 1925, but the track was destroyed by a hurricane in

1926, and the rebuilding process was not complete until 1930). Upon its opening, the track was recognized as one of the most appealing in the nation. It featured a well-appointed grandstand and clubhouse, as well as a small lake in the infield, which attracted flocks of flamingos. More importantly, the track was operated during the winter months, making it a popular winter destination for northern-based thoroughbred owners and trainers who were looking for warm weather in which to train their horses. Additionally, the track was able to collect large gambling revenues from the winter snowbirds who routinely vacationed in Florida.

For the first ten years or so of operation, Hialeah Park ruled the south Florida racing scene. But then, in 1939, Gulfstream Park opened, and of course, it wanted a cut of the racing revenue, which meant sharing those coveted winter racing dates that Hialeah Park had grown accustomed to having. Over the next several years, Gulfstream's management continuously requested better racing dates, to no avail.

Finally, in 1947, the Florida legislature had seen enough, and attempted to enact a new law that would fairly determine who was entitled to the most profitable racing dates. The problem with the statute was that it was unfair. The act provided that the track that generated the most revenue the previous year was given first choice of the racing dates for the upcoming year. It virtually guaranteed that because Hialeah already held the most lucrative racing dates, it would consistently be the most profitable track, and of course, it would always have the right to pick the same dates again the following year. Gulfstream Park challenged the new statute as a monopoly, and the case made it to the Florida Supreme Court, where Gulfstream ultimately lost. In upholding the case in favor of Hialeah, the court determined that the state of Florida had great discretion in allotting racing dates, because there was no true public interest or public welfare decision being made in the determination of the dates. The state's decision was not truly an exercise of the police power; that is, the state was not required to work within specific constitutional bounds.

Although clearly not happy about the decision, the Gulfstream Park management soldiered on with the less desirable racing dates. Then, in 1968, Gulfstream challenged again. This time, the results were drastically different. In a reversal of its own previous decision, the Florida Supreme Court determined that Hialeah's constant ability to operate during the coveted dates amounted to a violation of due process and equal protection. Further, the court determined that as a result of routinely awarding the best dates to Hialeah, the state had made Gulfstream the ongoing target of discrimination. In so finding, the court overturned the legislature's "Hialeah Bill" and restored the power to determine racing dates to the Florida State Racing Commission.

Unfortunately, the problem was not resolved. Numerous hearings were held to determine which track was entitled to the coveted dates, and ultimately, the state once again awarded the dates to Hialeah. The decision was premised largely on Hialeah's history as well as on its quality facilities for handling large racing crowds. As one can guess, Gulfstream's management was incensed and once again filed suit. The Florida State Supreme Court blasted the racing commission, and although its opinion did not specifically state so, it essentially ordered that those winter dates in question be awarded to Gulfstream.

Now, Hialeah found itself on the outside looking in. When the state racing commission again awarded the prime racing dates to Gulfstream for a second year, Hialeah took a page from Gulfstream's playbook, and filed suit itself. After a long procedural battle, the ultimate effect of this new challenge was to set up a rotational system, thereby giving each track the coveted dates every other year.

Unfortunately, the long battle had cost Hialeah too much. Hialeah Park's inability to maintain the premier mid-winter racing dates caused it to lose patrons and, ultimately, it could not afford to keep its gates open. The track ended live thoroughbred racing in 2001.

Interestingly, because the track had been listed on the National Register of Historic Places in 1979, it could not be destroyed. As such, rumors of Hialeah Park's resurrection have continued since its closing. In 2009, the track, in conjunction with the Seminole Tribe of Florida, was given permission to operate slot machines and host live quarter horse racing. The track recently began this live quarter horse racing, and rumors continue to circulate that a return of thoroughbred racing is not far off.

If a return of thoroughbred racing does happen, you can be assured that the legal fight will continue, and the racing dates will once again be brought into question.

Index

Index

Index

Index

About the Authors

Charles Palmer has been bedeviled by slow horses all his life. Growing up with such luminaries as Anderson G who showed "tremendous potential" in training but, sadly, never could beat anybody on the race track, Palmer learned to be patient and endure. Those traits have been horse racing's principal contribution to his career and only contribution to his bank account.

When not vainly rooting for slow horses, Palmer attended the University of Michigan Business School and Law School. He then went on to litigate various cases in the mid-Michigan area, including murder and personal injury cases.

In 1988, Palmer became a professor at the Thomas M. Cooley Law School teaching Torts, Property, Contracts, Art Law, Pretrial Litigation, and numerous other legal subjects. He has also taught law in Melbourne, Australia; Hamilton, New Zealand; Florence, Italy; Barcelona, Spain; and London, England. But the horses have always had their allure.

Palmer saw Secretariat win the Kentucky Derby, Sea the Stars win the Epsom Derby, and a passionate Italian kid win the Palio. He also climbed Mt. Kilimanjaro and ran with the bulls in Pamplona.

Palmer is the father of three sons, one of whom is the co-author of this book. They may be his greatest accomplishment.

Robert Palmer is an associate attorney at the law firm of Sinas, Dramis, Brake, Boughton & McIntyre, in Lansing, MI, where his practice focuses on personal injury and criminal law. He holds a juris doctorate degree from the Thomas M. Cooley Law School, and a Bachelor of Science in Agriculture and Natural Resource Communications from Michigan State University.

Rob has been infatuated with race horses all of his life, and has, at various points, been licensed by the State of Michigan as both a race horse owner and a racing groom. He and his wife Summer have traveled the world to attend horse races, including the

Kentucky Derby, the Belmont Stakes, the Epsom Derby, Folkestone, and numerous racetracks throughout Australia. He currently lives on his family's farm in Leslie, Michigan, with his wife Summer, his daughter Georgia, two dogs, two horses, two goats, and several barn cats. He is proud to say that his daughter is the fourth generation of Palmers to live on the farm.